POLITICAL DYNASTY IN MANDALUYONG CITY, PHILIPPINES

Philippine Research Colloquium Volume 8

JESSA MAE P. ALERA
GERALDINE G. DELOS REYES
ERA R. ISAGON
EMA P. MENDOZA
FLORENZEL P. RAGUNTON

POLITICAL DYNASTY IN MANDALUYONG CITY, PHILIPPINES

Philippine Research Colloquium Volume 8

GALDA VERLAG 2018

Bibliografische Information der Deutschen Nationalbibliothek
Die Deutsche Nationalbibliothek verzeichnet diese Publikation in der Deutschen Nationalbibliografie; detaillierte bibliografische Daten sind im Internet über http://dnb.ddb.de abrufbar.

© 2018 Galda Verlag, Glienicke
Neither this book nor any part may be reproduced or transmitted in any form or by any means electronic or mechanical, including photocopying, micro-filming, and recording, or by any information storage or retrieval system, without prior permission in writing from the publisher. Direct all inquiries to Galda Verlag, Franz-Schubert-Str. 61, 16548 Glienicke, Germany

ISBN 978-3-96203-035-3 (Print)
ISBN 978-3-96203-036-0 (Ebook)

Originally presented as the authors thesis at the College Department of Political Science, Rizal Technological University, Manila, 2018

ACKNOWLEDGEMENTS

The researchers' great appreciation goes to several individuals whom in one way or another have made this research possible. They would like to extend their utmost gratitude and sincerest appreciation to the following:

Dr. Elmer Martin, Prof. Michael Mesinas, and Prof. Nouvie Aguirre, for their efforts in validating the thesis questionnaires. They also provided improvement on the instrument of the study;

The Honorable Barangay Chairmen of 25 Barangays of Mandaluyong City and their Staffs, for accommodating the researchers in conducting a survey in their respective barangays;

The Voters and Residents of Mandaluyong City, for giving their time and patiently answering the survey questionnaires;

Mr. Neil Adrian Pastrana, for accompanying the researchers to the different barangays for the survey;

Rizal Technological University CAS Library, for the books and computer resources used in their study and for borrowing the researchers to stay in the library premises from the beginning until the completion of the study;

Dr. Virginia Sobremisana, the researchers' thesis professor, for her never ending support and guidance throughout the whole research. Also, for her willingness and dedication to help the researchers until completion of the study;

Prof. Vanessa Umali, the researchers' thesis adviser, for her outstanding effort of encouragement, dedication and patience in editing and correcting the research study and for sharing her knowledge as well as guiding the researchers all throughout this study;

To the Researchers' Family, who gave moral and financial support to pursue this study and also for their undying love, guidance and words of encouragement;

And, of course, to Almighty God, who bestowed the clarity of the heart and mind to finish this study and making all things possible, thus glory and praise be given unto Him.

J.M.P.A.
G.G.D.R.
E.R.I.
E.P.M.
F.P.R.

ABSTRACT

Political dynasties have been present in democracies, raising concerns that inequality in the distribution of political power may reflect imperfections in democratic representation. However, the persistence of political elites may simply reflect differences in ability or political vocation across political families and not their entrenchment in power. Political Dynasty is a family in which several members are involved in politics, particularly electoral politics. Philippines is a democratic country where people have the right to choose government officials they want. People have the power to elect them without the intervention of others.

This study was conducted to know the perception of the people of Mandaluyong regarding political dynasty. The quantitative research answered the questions about the reasons why political dynasty exists and its positive and negative effects. The researchers also identified the strategies to regulate political dynasty. Aside from that, the researchers will also know why people choose the same officials. Are they aware of what political dynasty is? Does political dynasty limit the rights of an individual to be elected in a position in the government? If ever political dynasty would be regulated, does it also limit the rights of political families to run in a government position? This study will answer these questions based on perceptions of selected voters of Mandaluyong City.

TABLE OF CONTENTS

Acknowledgements v
Abstract ix

1 THE PROBLEM AND ITS BACKGROUND

Introduction 1

Theoretical Framework 2

Statement of the Problem 5

Hypothesis 6

Significance of the Study 6

Definition of Terms 7

2 REVIEW OF RELATED LITERATURE

Political Dynasty 9

Emergence of Political Dynasties 10

Causes of Existence of Political Dynasty 11

Effects of Political Dynasty 12

Consequences of Dynasties in Democracies 13

Political Dynasty in the Philippines 14

Political Machinery 15

Political Competition 16

Political Term 17

Politics and Poverty 19

Political History of Mandaluyong City 21

Synthesis 23

3 RESEARCH METHODOLOGY

Research Method Used 25

Population Frame and Sampling Scheme 25

Description of the Respondents 25

Instrument 26

Data Gathering Procedure 26

Statistical Treatment 26

4 PRESENTATION, ANALYSIS AND INTERPRETATION OF DATA

Presentation, Analysis and Interpretation of Data 29

5 SUMMARY OF FINDINGS, CONCLUSIONS, AND RECOMMENDATIONS

Summary of Findings 77

Conclusions 79

Recommendations 80

References 81

Appendices 83

1
THE PROBLEM AND ITS BACKGROUND

This chapter deals with the study of the problem and its background. Specifically it includes the introduction, statement of the problem, conceptual framework, the significance of the study, scope and delimitation, and the definition of terms used.

Introduction

Political dynasty is a succession of people from the same family who plays a role in politics. They are typically characterized as families that have established their political or economic dominance (Simbulan, 2007).

Members of a political dynasty may be related by blood or marriage; often several generations or multiple siblings may be involved, establishing their political or economic dominance in a province and or in a city. They have the superiority in the Philippine politics both national and local levels have been there for at least three decades.

Political dynasty has advantages and disadvantages that may affect the community and the people as well. One of the advantages of that since they have enough background on politics and well-versed in governance, since the same family is in government positions and know how to deal with the constituents.

Being familiar in leading people is a good factor. Also, people vote these political families to improve their lives. This is a good thing especially if the family has a good track record in their services and maintains integrity in the government posistion.

The Anti-Dynasty Bill has made it to the public's knowledge but there are also opposing ideas the settled within the place of discussion. Those who consider dynasties as part of the Philippine Elections say that banning political clans is not the solution, the proper way to settle it is to educate the people, the voters on how to responsibly utilize their power to choose who deserves the seat of influence (Enriquez, 2015).

Political dynasty emanates basically from three factors: (1) the political and socio-economic foundations upon which political dynasties are built; 2) the inability to effectively implement Philippine constitutional provisions by enacting an enabling law; and 3) the weakness of potential countervailing forces that would challenge political dynasties. The resilience of the established political dynasties across the decades was in great part due to their ability to diversify economically, enabling them to adapt and hold on to their political power. At the same time, for new dynasties, the accumulation of a diversity of economic interests means that a small dynasty can emerge from even the poorest provinces of the country (Tadem, 2016).

The study aims to discover why political dynasty continues to exist and its advantages and disadvantages as perceived by the residents of Mandaluyong City in order to find the answers toward the attitudes of the respondents.

Theoretical Framework

In the theory of elite socialization, scholars believe that members of political dynasties are more exposed than others to a conducive environment for internalization of particular political values, education on how to run political strategies, and getting used to with life as a politician. Thus, members of political dynasties naturally want to follow the career path of their forerunner. In some societies, a family becomes a primary channel for elite selection and recruitment. According to Michels (1999), the tendency of elites to keep up themselves in power persists across time.

A famous theory by Mancur Olson notes that even less compassionate leaders with a secure hold on power may behave like a 'stationary bandits', benefit from their position yet ensuring that growth and development nevertheless take place in order to continue to secure their hold.

This research has two theories. First is the Public Choice Theory (James Buchanan in The Calculus of Consent, 1964). It argues that economic self-interest is the driving force of politics. People will vote for the candidate that they believe is going to give them the greatest access to more money. Second is the Rational Choice Theory (Anthony Downs, 1957). It is an economic principle that states that individuals always make prudent and logical decisions. These decisions provide people with the greatest benefit or satisfaction – given the choices available – and are also in their highest self-interest. This theory maintains that "when faced with several courses of actions, people usually do what they believe is likely to have the best overall outcome" (Elster, 1989 in Ward, 2002). In a similar vein, rational choice institutionalism – a variation of rational choice theory – argued that political institutions influence behavior (Huntington, 1968; Goodin, 1966) affecting the structure of a situation in which individuals select strategies for the pursuit of their preferences (Ostrom, 1982).

If applied to political behavior or voting, these theories may be able to provide an explanation why voters, especially the poor and illiterate ones, tend to favor or support politicians who are able to provide public services in a personalized and individual manner regardless of the fact that they only derived short-term benefits.

Thus, using these theories as a guide, the study will attempt to demonstrate that political behavior or electoral choice is largely structured or shaped by the situation in which people, in this study find themselves. It has been argued that individual political behavior is largely a function of social structures. As such, social class, geographic location, gender, consumption and production, location and religion, among other variables, all have known correlations, of greater or lesser strength, with voting behavior (Harrop & Miller, 1987).

4 . THE PROBLEM AND ITS BACKGROUND

PUBLIC CHOICE THEORY	STATIONARY BANDITS
a body of theory developed by James Buchanan and Gordon Tullock to try to explain how public decisions are made. It involves the interaction of the voting public, the politicians, the bureaucracy and political action committees.	A government behaves like a stationary bandit only if it is confident of its continued reign. When citizens aren't sure of a government's stability, the government can't credibly commit to long-term protection of property and contract rights (which means less investment/growth); to overcome this problem, kings establish dynastic succession orders.

Reasons Why People Choose Political Families
Based on Two Theories
Figure 1

Public Choice Theory argues that economic self-interest is the driving force of politics. People will vote for the candidate that they believe is going to give them the greatest access to more money.

Stationary bandit monopolizes and rationalizes theft in the form of taxes and tyrant who has an incentive to encourage some degree of economic success as he expects to remain in power long enough to benefit from that success.

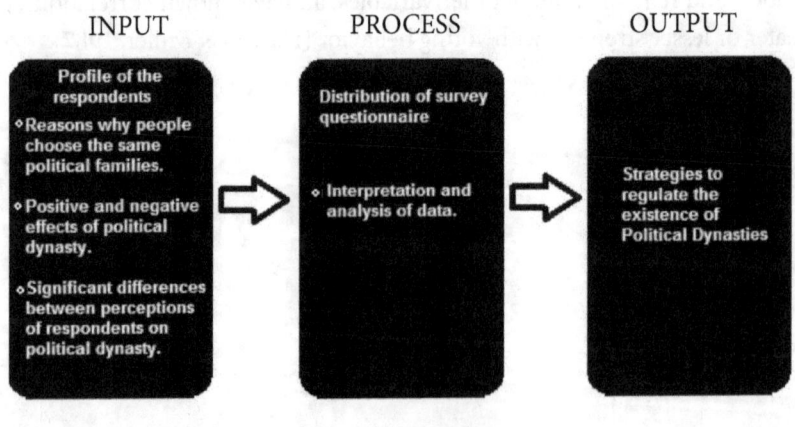

Research Paradigm
Figure 2

The structure of this research paradigm adopted the input-process-output paradigm. This paradigm shows the direction of the research. First, the researchers identified the profile of the respondents. Then, the researchers gathered the reasons why people choose the same political families, the positive and negative effects of political dynasty and the significant differences between their perceptions from the respondents. The purpose of this study is to know the perceptions of residents towards political dynasty, reasons of existence and the strategies to regulate political dynasty. The researchers distributed survey questionnaire to the respondents in order to gather data and interpret and analyze them afterwards.

Statement of the Problem

1. What is the demographic profile of the respondent in terms of
    1.1 Age;
        1.1.a.) 18-35 years old
        1.1.b.) 36-45 years old
        1.1.c.) 46 years old and above
    1.2 Gender;
        1.2.a.) Female
        1.2.b.) Male
    1.3 Monthly income
        1.3.a.) 10,000 and below
        1.3.b.) 11,000 to 20,000
        1.3.c.) 21,000 and above
2. What are the reasons why people choose the same political families?
3. What are the effects of existence of Political Dynasty?
    3.1 Positive Effects
        3.1.a.) Provides stability
        3.1.b.) Experienced Politicians
        3.1.c.) Knowledge on politics
        3.1.d.) Good economic performance
        3.1.e.) Long term programs
        3.1.f.) Hones an aspiring leader
    3.2 Negative Effects
        3.2.a.) Corruption
        3.2.b.) Tyranny

3.2.c.) Dirty Politics
3.2.d.) Limiting other's chance
3.2.e.) Poverty
4. What strategies can be adapted to regulate the existence of Political Dynasty?

Hypothesis

There are significant differences on the perceived reason why people choose same political families by profile. Political dynasty exists because of gratitude at the same time money, trust, knowedge, popularity and social status of the candidates by profile.

Aside from that, there are positive and negative impact on the perceived effects of the existence of poitical dynasty by profile.

Significance of the Study

The researchers believe that this research study will help them spread more information on the constant issue here in the Philippines which is the political dynasty. The researchers will look at how political dynasty affects communities specifically in Mandaluyong City. The study will benefit the following:

Students in Mandaluyong City. The study will provide them knowledge about political dynasties and its members in Mandaluyong City, even in neighboring cities.

Citizens in Mandaluyong City. The study will give them information on how political dynasty affects their community in positive and negative ways.

Voters in Mandaluyong City. The study will help them decide on who to vote in the upcoming elections.

Aspiring Politicians. The study will give them knowledge on how families of politicians help the city and what projects can help improve their community.

Lawmakers. The study will enlighten them in defining and elaborating Political Dynasty in the Philippines.

Scope and Delimitation

The main focus of this study is to know the advantages and disadvantages of the political dynasty and the reasons for its existence as perceived by the residents of Mandaluyong City. The researcher will conduct a survey to the twenty-five barangays in Mandaluyong City. And will select twenty (20) registered voters in each barangay to complete the five hundred (500) respondents to represent and identify the result of the study. A survey questionnaire is used to answer the questions that are related to the objected study, in order to make graphs and charts to represent the analysis. The name of respondents is optional.

Definition of Terms

It is appropriate to define terms to identify some terms for better understanding before the conduct of the review of literature. The terms that bring highlight in this study were given emphasis by defining it operationally and hypothetically.

Authoritarian Regime refers to a government that concentrates political power in an authority not responsible to the people. The authoritarian regime is the governing authority of a political unit.

Democracy is a form of government based on the sovereignty of people. An organization or situation in which everyone is treated equally and has equal rights is called democracy.

Democratization is a transition to a more democratically regime; to make it possible for all people to understand something.

Political Dynasty refers to a family in which several members are involved in politics.

Political Landscape refers to the current state of thing, as well as how they are looking in the future.

Political Power is the ability to influence or outright control the behavior.

Political Violence means violence outside of the state control that is politically violated.

Public Interest is a common concern among citizen in the management and affairs of state, local and national government.

Social Class is the division of a society based on social and economic aspects.

2
REVIEW OF RELATED LITERATURE

This part of the study will be discussing the relevant literature connected with the study of the political dynasty, its pros and cons and reasons of existence. This part of the study accounts works that have been published on the topic by accredited scholars and researchers.

Political Dynasty

As defined by Sue Nyathi, a political dynasty is a group of families that remain in position or power in a country for many generations or has a succession of leaders from the same family. Previous studies define political dynasties in various ways.

Dal Bó et al. (2009) define political dynasty "those from a family that had previously placed a member in Congress." Ishibashi and Reed (1992) and Asako et al. (2012) define political dynasty simply as a group of politicians who inherit public office from one of their family members who occupy the office. In the same manner, Thompson (2012) describes political dynasties as another type of direct and indirect political power shift involving family members. Additionally, Querubin (2011) defines a political dynasty as one or a small number of families who dominate the power distribution in a certain geographic area.

In his earlier work, Querubin (2010) defines a dynastic politician as someone who has family members who served as a member of Congress or Governor prior to the election. This study argues that political dynasties are not merely about continuation but also include spreading out of power to other branches of autonomous institutions (for instance, legislative or executive branches at lower or higher levels). For instance, if A is a governor of a province and A's family member B is a member of that province's parliament, then the definition set by Asako et al. is unable to capture this phenomenon as a political dynasty. Their definition applies only if A is a governor and B directly replaces A in a subsequent election.

Emergence of Political Dynasties

The occurrence of political dynasties was believed to be recorded in the pre-Magellanic period. According to Renato Constantino's book "The making of a Filipino", he pointed out that "Communities at this time were already accustomed to an early form of government and politics". He also said that the strong familial bonds espoused the development of leadership and social prestige in this ruling class. In the Pre-colonial society, we have the datu, raja and the maharlika as rulers and stewards of ethnic communities. Nevertheless, the datu, raja, and maharlika class served as the framework for the formation of political dynasties in the Philippines.

When the Spanish occupation where the term principalia was introduced which determines the person who leads. In Constantino's perception, "The principalia was composed of the wealthy landowners, many of whom were descendants of the early datus and maharlikas" (Constantino, 1969). During this time, the datu has been entrusted with fiscal and administrative duties and became adjuncts of Spanish power, from mere administrators of socially-owned properties during the pre-Magellanic period. Then, the principalia became formal owners of the lands and along with the mestizos, illustrados, mestizo-sangley, creole, and Chinese mestizos created the local oligarchs of the country.

In the study of Temario Rivera "In Landlords and Capitalists', he revealed that almost eighty-seven (87) families are controlling the top one hundred and twenty (120) manufacturing companies from 1964 to 1986 (Rivera, 1994). at about twenty percent of these families were involved in politics and most of them were members of the landowning elite that emerged during the 19th century, including the Aranetas, Cojuangcos, Jacintos, Madrigals, and Yulos. To Rivera, "the land capitalists caused the diversion of state resources to traditional elite economic activities like sugar and coconut milling, limiting further industrial diversification" where the government was influenced.

Those elites capitalize on education to innovate ideas and information. For Pierre Bourdieu, a French sociologist which he calls "The cultural capital", the local and national elites acquired a new form of a mechanism through education. It is the way to election participation and a prerogative of wealth. in the history, the elections were only catered to the elites, which comprises less than one percent of the population of the community. William Howard Taft led the first ever election which limits the number of participants to the local and national elites.

Causes of Existence of Political Dynasty

According to Acemoglu et. al., political dynasty existed for the influential families who want the power inside the government. Dynastic politicians come from diverse occupational backgrounds (often business) and run for once as a means of consolidating their economic standing and the political power of the dynasty (Coronel et. al., 2007; Fafchamps and Labonne, 2015). Studies by Camp (1976) in Mexico and Mendoza (2012) on Philippine dynastic politics suggest that the rise of political dynasties can be attributed in part to traditional societies and poor economic conditions under which voters with lower economic status tend to vote for dynastic politicians. Furthermore, the failure of political parties in establishing democratic intra-party selection and promotion mechanisms has provided fertile ground for dynastic politicians to dominate the decision making within the party organization, including to nurture, promote, and select the party's candidates for elections.

Studies by Chhibber (2013) in India, Harjanto (2011) in Indonesia, and Amundsen (2013) in Bangladesh propose the similar argument that poor party institutionalization is the culprit that paves a way for dynastic politicians to capture nomination of the party's candidate for elections.

The rampant political dynasty building today was described by Tuazon as tactics of "self-preservation and expansion, which are means for a continuing rule of political dynasties." For instance, the 2013 senatorial slates are basically coalitions of political dynasties through party-switching for networking and political preservation. Image and visual packaging have become key factors in the expansion, preservation, and continuing rule of political dynasties. Partnerships with lawyers, the media, showbiz personalities, and corporations have favored wider expansion and greater popularity for these political dynasties, ensuring their rule over Philippine politics.

Effects of Political Dynasty

As in the case of family-run norms, the existence of dynastic leaders raises the question of whether they are good for economic performance at the country level or bad as Besley and Querol (2014) said. Moreover, it is often felt dynasties promote politics of self-serving interests and non-equitable distribution of resources and opportunities as said by Sue Nyathi (2014). Political dynasties (Paterno, 2014) present a greater threat to democracy when much of them control the majority of power in the country. She (Paterno, 2014) said that various members of the same family often cycle through the same political positions in their provinces, cities and other political areas.

Acemoglu and Robinson (2008) emphasize the way by which elite persistence may undermine attempts to reform institutions, leading to captured democracies wherein economic institutions and policies disproportionately benefit the elite. Political dynasties can undermine the quality of democracy and economic development in the long growth. Mendoza, et al. (2012) found evidence that political dynasties in the 15th Congress won by much larger margins of victory, and tended to be wealthier. Nevertheless, they found that Philippine provinces with higher levels of political dynasties also displayed higher levels of poverty and weaker indicators of human development.

A Center for People Empowerment in Governance (CenPEG) study in 2011 showed that the May 2010 elections—during which the automated election system was used nationwide for the first time—increased, even more, the number of political dynasties both at the national and local levels. Political dynasties have been thriving with memberships increasing through horizontal and vertical expansion. For instance, in the 15th Congress, vertical and horizontal expansion included local and national positions, covering legislative districts, provinces, and regions, and even penetrating the party-list system.

Political dynasties might also result in positive effects for gender representation, as dynastic succession may be one way for female candidates to break into politics in systems where women are otherwise disadvantaged (Jalazai, 2013; Folke et al. 2016). Indeed, many female politicians in the U.S. and elsewhere first entered politics when their husbands died in office, a process sometimes referred to as a 'widow's succession' (Kincaid, 1978). Folke et al. (2016) argue that political dynasties are beneficial for female representation in politics because they help voters and party actors involved in candidate selection overcome information asymmetries with respect to the quality of female candidates. Their empirical analysis combines comparative legislator-level data from twelve democracies and candidate-level data from Ireland and Sweden and provides strong evidence that political dynasties' positive effects for gender representation indeed arise because they allow women to overcome a voting disadvantage in elections.

Consequences of Dynasties in Democracies

Understanding the causes of dynasties establishes a necessary precondition for studying their potential socio-economic consequences. For instance, political dynasties caused by assortative matching between spouses might have very different implications than political dynasties arising due to, for example, rent-seeking motivations. Yet, in stark contrast to research on family firms – where the discussion has largely centered on 'whether family owned firms have advantages in the marketplace' (Besley, 2005) – few studies have thus far addressed the potential consequences of political dynasties. As argued by Besley (2005), the 'advantage in name recognition is palpable [but] whether politician quality is transmitted intergenerationally is far from clear'. What are the political and economic consequences of political dynasties? Do dynasties generate positive or negative effects on the functioning of democracy or the quality of representation?

On one hand, if dynastic politicians enjoy advantages which shield them from electoral accountability, it might result in a decrease in the quality of representation. Much like female legislators in the U.S. must outperform their male counterparts to overcome higher barriers to entry (Anzia and Berry, 2011) and female members of parliament in Germany require more political experience to obtain extra-parliamentary jobs (Geys and Mause, 2014), non-dynastic candidates who run against dynastic candidates might need to be of higher quality, and exhibit higher legislative performance if elected. This means that dynastic politicians might be of lower quality in terms of policymaking, even if they are of higher quality in terms of electoral strength. This may be particularly troubling since dynastic politicians appear to enjoy an advantage over other MPs in progressing from the backbenches to the cabinet (Smith and Martin, 2016), placing them at the pinnacle of political leadership.

On the other hand, dynasties might also have a positive effect on democracy. For example, Parker (1996) argues that members of dynasties may be beneficial to the functioning of the legislature, since 'family members who have served in Congress can act in a tutorial capacity'. The electoral advantages that dynastic politicians possess may also translate into downstream distributive advantages for their districts. Dynastic politicians elected on their personal reputation might, for instance, be more motivated to provide benefits to their districts than politicians who owe their election to their party label alone. This would reflect Keefer and Khemani's (2009) argument that legislator effort at 'bringing home the pork' is lower in constituencies where party identification among voters is stronger.

Daniele and Vertier (2016) analyze a large sample of Italian mayors in the period 1998-2013 and find no effects of dynastic mayors on average spending, revenue, and transfer levels. They do find, however, that dynastic mayors tend to implement stronger political budget cycles. In contrast, Besley and Reynal-Querol (2015) present evidence that dynastic leaders may positively impact the rate of economic growth, but only where the leader enjoys significant autonomy in decision-making.

Clearly, there may be multiple ways, both direct and indirect, in which dynastic politics can have consequences for socio-economic outcomes and the quality of representation in a democracy. For instance, it might be that dynastic politicians are more constrained by their family than non-dynastic politicians – leading to less change in public policies following dynastic succession. This argument is consistent with Besley and Reynal- Querol's (2015) finding that individuals' autonomy in decision-making represents a crucial mediating factor to observe differences in socio-economic outcomes between jurisdictions run by dynastic and non-dynastic leaders. Yet, overall, the mechanisms linking political dynasties and their possible consequences for socio-economic outcomes remain poorly understood. Moreover, establishing the causal connection between dynasties and their socioeconomic consequences is challenging due to the many confounding factors at play.

Political Dynasty in the Philippines

Political dynasties continue their supremacy in the Philippine political landscape, especially in isolated and far-off provinces, despite anti-dynasty initiatives of civil society (Ronda, 2013). Political dynasty, as defined by a number of analysts, is a family which each member either by blood or marriage is in politics or in other positions as a public servant. In Senate

Bill 2649, which was made and introduced by Senator Santiago, the political family is practiced by a family of incumbent elective officials and powers are distributed in different positions in the government.

In the Philippines, the political dynasty has been the topic of growing number of studies. The emergence and persistence of political dynasties from the unequal socio-economic structure of Philippine society results to lack of development to the democratic electoral and party system of the country (Teehankee, 2007). The unfitness of the majority to repugn the elite is argued to get numerous political dynasties. Sidel (1997) says that the politicians in the Philippines give some money to gain supporters in the political campaign to compete with electoral fraud and vote buying. Political success, on the other hand, allows resources and opportunities to enable political dynasty for the expansion of their economic and power bases (McCoy, 1994).

The background of the elites becomes powerful when people support them. These elite legislators enjoy their reign as a public servant. The perception of citizens to these issues is still important to know how people understand political dynasty, regardless of race, gender, and economic class. (Guarde, et.al. 2016)

Querubin (2010) thinks about all congressional and gubernatorial applicants between 1946 furthermore, 2007 in the Philippines. He finds that barely winning a race builds the likelihood of having a relative entering office by around fifteen to twenty-two percent.

Political Machinery

Political success requires political machinery that is why wealth and popularity are not needed to create political dynasties. Coronel (2007) therefore argues that the contingency on the creation of political network equal to rebuilding wealth and influence into votes are needed for a successful political campaign. Coronel said that through mergers, the political dynasties often consolidate their powers.

In contrast, Sidel adds that because of their affiliation with more powerful political entities, several dynasties succeed. Thus, to draw upon larger pools of resources and broaden their political influence, forging alliances with the larger and more powerful political families enables prospective political dynasties. To complement their advantages or compensate for their disadvantages with the systemic use of violence and intimidation, some political dynasties are also known. The long history of politically motivated assassinations argues that violence provides some dynastic politicians the opportunity to remove or grievously cripple the rival political dynasties.

On the Philippine Congress, recent analyses cohere with the earlier studies. Querubin (2010), for instance, stated that the estimated number of legislators of Filipino with the capacity for self-perpetuation of is three times higher than those legislators in the United States. Meanwhile, Balisacan and Fuwa (2004) uncover evidence that the presence of political dynasties influences the growth in expenditure but not the reduction in poverty. In addition, they find that political dynasties are negatively associated with subsequent income.

Voters may incline toward dynastic possibility for various reasons. The most instinctive one is name acknowledgment. Voters may lean toward applicants who share a surname with an established legislator. For dynastic hopefuls the brand of their surname can help to flag their political quality. Dynastic applicants can likewise have different points of interest to prescribe them to voters. For the US, Feinstein (2010) gauges a brand name advantage for dynastic competitors of around 0.7 to 8 rate purposes of the aggregate vote in races for the US Congress and Senate. The approach in this paper of contrasting applicant surnames with the surnames of past lawmakers over these levels, can in this way be relied upon to distinguish a significant number of the politically dynamic families.

Besides name recognition and networks, wealth would seem to be an important supply-side factor in explaining dynastic persistence. Bohlken and Chandra (2013) investigate dynasties in India and ask to what extent dynastic success can be explained by the party's promotion of these candidates. They find that dynastic candidates with relatives in politics before them are more likely to be re-nominated by their parties, and when they are re-nominated by their parties they also receive a higher vote share in the election. They argue that party organization matters.

Sequential dynasties (dynasties whose members follow one another but do not serve together) are more prominent in the parties with weak leadership, while concurrent dynasties are more common in parties with strong leadership.

Political Competition

By incumbency advantage, a large body of theoretical literature emphasizes the barriers to entry created. The rules of political competition (such as redistricting) and tend to spend more money on campaigning than challengers (Abramowitz, 1991) control by incumbents in order to determine.

Similarly, Lott (1986) develops a model wherein investments in a political brand name are non-transferable constituting past campaign expenditures as a barrier to the entry of new challenges. Other scholars argue that incumbency advantage mutes the beneficial effect of competitive elections, allows incumbents to disregard the interests of the electorate, and prevents the entry of potentially more productive politicians.

Term limits eliminate incumbency advantage periodically, possibly increasing the number of open seats for new politicians from different parties, coalitions, or political sectors who are unlikely to enter office in races with an incumbent. This will increase rotation in power and could potentially eliminate the biases of policy in favor of the coalitions that long-serving incumbents represent (Tabarrok, 1996 and Cain, Hanley and Kousser, 2001).

Rotation in office is particularly important in the context of risk-averse voters with very heterogeneous preferences who would benefit from term limits that prevent the entrenchment of an opposing group in 3See Benjamin and Malbin (1992), p.20-21. 6 power for a long time (Glaeser, 1997 and Tabarrok, 1996).

Shugart, Valdini and Suominen (2005) contend that nearby hopefuls have simply such favorable positions. So also, dynastic status could give voters extra data. The apparent political nature of the senior dynastic legislator can be used to induce the political nature of the lesser applicant.

Political Term

Term limits go back to early vote based social orders. In creating nations, for example, Colombia, the Philippines, and Venezuela, sacred changes have been passed keeping in mind the end goal to alter (or expel) term restrictions on the president and other chose authorities. In the scholarly writing, the exchange for or against term limits has typically focused around two fundamental contentions: expanding office pivot by killing incumbency advantage also, expelling long-residency officeholders from office. A huge assortment of hypothetical writing accentuates the hindrances to section made by incumbency advantage.

Occupants control the establishments that decide the guidelines of political rivalry, and have a tendency to spend more cash on crusading than challengers (Abramowitz, 1991). Term limits dispose of incumbency advantage intermittently, conceivably expanding quantities of open seats for new government officials from various gatherings, coalitions, or political parties who are improbable to enter office in races with an officeholder. This will expand turn in control and could possibly wipe out the predispositions of strategy for the coalitions that long-serving incumbents speak to (Tabarrok, 1996 and Cain, Hanley and Kousser, 2001). Turn in office is especially essential with regards to chance loath voters with extremely heterogeneous inclinations who might profit by term confines that keep the entrenchment of a contradicting bunch in control for quite a while (Glaeser, 1997 and Tabarrok, 1996).

As an outcome, voters lean toward a delegate who is generally senior and can all the more effectively representative assets and enactment to profit her own constituents. While voters may profit by having an alternate and more gainful delegate, no single constituency will do it singularly in light of the fact that they relinquish relative residency and net exchanges. In this setting, Dick and Lott (1993) build up a model in which term limits break this balance and enable voters to pick better hopefuls by breaking the rank of all local simultaneously.

Normally, huge numbers of these contentions must be differentiated against the organization writing, most strikingly Barro (1973), that accentuates the restraining part of decisions and talks about the crafty conduct in which term-restricted officeholders draw in amid their last period, once reelection motivations vanish. The exact writing on the outcomes of term limits is all the rarer and core interests exclusively in the United States.

At first, a group of writing utilized recreation models in light of past reelection rates to foresee the impact of term restricts on the pivot of energy and the piece of the governing body. For example, Fowler (1992) and Grofman and Sutherland (1996) contend that term cut-off points may expand the re-election rates of officeholders since high caliber challengers put off running until the point that the seat winds up noticeably open by required turn.

Cain, Hanley and Kousser (2001) find that seats held by occupants are less inclined to be challenged and that officeholders tend to confront challenges with less past political experience. Specifically, past work has not investigated observationally the degree to which running for an alternate office or, on the other hand substitution by relatives can undermine the viability of term limits. This is especially important with regards to dynastic or first class commanded majority rule governments, where individual or gathering turnover is not really the pertinent measure of intrigue, yet rather the degree to which political foundations can break the restraining infrastructure of effective families and increment the differing qualities of interests spoke to.

Politics and Poverty

A recent study reveals the influence of social and political factors on the amount of poverty in a county. According to Stephan Goetz, director of the Northeast Regional Center for Rural Development and Penn State professor of agricultural and regional economics, economic factors can partially explain the variation in poverty rates among regions, but they cannot give the full picture. He also added that some anti-poverty policies focus on improving the educational level of the residents and creating new jobs, but those strategies do not automatically guarantee change in the poverty rate.

Schaffer (2002) studied the practice of vote buying in the Philippines, and his analysis revealed how low-income voters tend to prefer candidates and political groups that show respect and a degree of compassion to the low-income population. Thus, the advocacies of middle-class groups and stakeholders that have used advertisements and leaflets to advocate against vote selling are often regarded as patronizing by low-income voters. Indeed, as Schaffer (2002) argues, these voters do not see themselves as selling their votes. It is possible that political dynasties have mastered the art of supporting poor and vulnerable communities, while still showing a measure of respect and compassion that low-income voters appreciate. This view is in sharp contrast to the non-dynastic and progressive groups, which typically advance the messages of empowerment, self-help and voter responsibility.

Ravanilla (2012) finds evidence that political dynasties may use public funds to support allies and clan members. His analysis of the disbursement of the constituent development fund (CDF) of legislators tends to favor local patrons, particularly mayoral partisan allies in their districts. Such a skewed allocation of resources could also potentially weaken the chances to attain policy objectives such as poverty reduction, as argued by Mendoza, et al. (2012). Hence, self-perpetuation and (less robust) poverty reduction outcomes may actually be linked, even as it appears that political patrons are trying to spend public funds in a "pro-poor" way.

Mayors of Mandaluyong City
Figure 3

Mayor	Year	Mayor	Year
Buenaventura Domingo	1901	Primo Guzman	1945
Antonio Fernando	1902	Bonifacio Javier	1946; 1947-1955; 1960-1962
Juanario Conorado	1902; 1909; 1912	Amado Reyes	1963
Miguel Vergara	1902	Filemon Javier	1964-1971
Pantaleon Blas	1903	Melchor Arcangel	1963
Claro Castaneda	1905	Macario Trinidad	1963
Apolinar Coronado	1907; 1909	Renato Lopez	1972-1980
Marcelo Lerma	1912-1916	Ernesto Domingo	1980-1986
Mariano Castaneda	1916-1922	Benjamin S. Abalos, Sr. (OIC)	1986-1987
Gregorio Pedro	1923-1926	Roman Delos Santos (OIC)	1987-1988
Clemente Fernando	1926-1934	Benjamin S. Abalos, Sr.	1988-1998
Isaac Lopez	1935-1939	Neptali M. Gonzales II	2004-2007
Ponciano Enriquez	1940	Benjamin S. Abalos, Jr.	1998-2004; 2007-2016
Pedro Cruz	1941; 1945; 1956-1959	Carmelita Aguilar-Abalos	2016- Present

List of the former and current Mayors of Mandaluyong city is enlisted on the table. It shows the transition of the dynasties present since 1900's. The Mayoral started by Former Mayor Buenaventura Domingo and the Current Mayor Charisse Abalos who is the daughter of Former Mayor Benjamin S. Abalos.

Political History of Mandaluyong City

Formerly called San Felipe Neri, Mandaluyong was once a barrio of Sta. Ana de Sapa, Province of Tondo, during the Spanish colonial rule. It was separated from Sta. Ana de Sapa in 1841 and established its own parish in 1863.

During the American regime, it became a first class municipality but was later consolidated with the municipality of San Juan del Monte under Presidential Act No. 942. For several months in 1904, it became the capital of the province of Rizal. It became an independent municipality by virtue of House Bill No. 3836 in 1907, and was officially named the Municipality of Mandaluyong.

At the onset of World War II, the municipality was occupied by the Japanese and later liberated by American forces on February 9, 1945. In the 1960's, following a period of reconstruction and development, it became a component municipality of the Greater Manila Area, which today is known as Metropolitan Manila.

On February 9, 1994, forty-nine years after its liberation from the Japanese, Mandaluyong has been converted into a highly urbanized city by virtue of Republic Act 7675 signed by then President Fidel V. Ramos.

Residents of Mandaluyong have always been known for their industry. Men did the laundry to the amusement of non-residents until shortly after the war, while the women ironed the clothes. These industrious people trace their roots to Emperor Soledan (also known as "Anka Widyaya" of the Great Madjapahit Empire) and Empress Sasaban of the Kingdom of Sapa whose son Prince Balagtas ruled as sovereign of the kingdom in about the year 1300.

More than a century later, in about the year 1470, it expanded and was called the "Kingdom of Namayan" with "Lakan Takhan" as sovereign. The vast Kingdom comprised what are now Quiapo, San Miguel, Sta. Mesa, Paco, Pandacan, Malate and Sta. Ana in Manila, and Mandaluyong, San Juan, Makati, Pasay, Pateros, Taguig, Parañaque, and portions of Pasig and Quezon City up to Diliman that were then part of Mandaluyong.

Mandaluyong was first known as a barrio of Sta. Ana de Sapa which was part of the District of Paco, Province of Tondo. Named San Felipe Neri by the Spaniards in honor of the Patron Saint of Rome, it was separated civilly from Sta. Ana de Sapa in 1841.

On September 15, 1863 San Felipe Neri established its own parish and under the administration of the Congregation "Dulcisimo Nombre de Jesus", it constructed its own church, convent and school.

The Parish of San Felipe Neri played a significant role as a relay station for propagating the Katipunan during the 1896-1898 Revolution. It was in Barangay Hagdang Bato on August 28, 1896 where Andres Bonifacion issued a proclamation setting Saturday, August 29, 1896 as the date of the attack on Manila. It was also in this town that the revolutionary paper, "La Republika", was established on September 15, 1896.

During the American regime, San Felipe Neri was raised to a first class municipality with five (5) barrios, namely: Poblacion, Barangka, Hagdang Bato, Namayan and Hulo. Under Presidential Act No. 942, it was consolidated with the municipality of San Juan del Monte and became the seat of government. For several months in 1904, San Felipe Neri became the capital of the province of Rizal.

San Felipe Neri was separated from San Juan and became an independent municipality on March 27, 1907. It was renamed the Municipality of Mandaluyong by virtue of House Bill No. 3836 which was authored and sponsored by Assemblyman Pedro Magsalin, then the Representative of the District of Rizal.

During World War II, Mandaluyong lost many of her people, among them were Catholic priests and civilians. Destruction was felt all over, but with the timely arrival of the American Liberation Forces on February 9, 1945, the municipality was saved from further damages. That day became a red calendar day for Mandaluyong marking its liberation from the Japanese Imperial forces by the Americans.

In the 60's, Mandaluyong became a component municipality of Metropolitan Manila. Together with other component cities and municipalities, it has undergone significant physical and economic transformation. From a forestal town to a progressive municipality, Mandaluyong is now a highly urbanized city known to host most of the country's best companies and corporations, shopping malls and hotels which are certainly world class in status. Mandaluyong and the municipality of San Juan used to be represented in congress by a single Congressman. As it entered cityhood in 1994, Mandaluyong became a lone district with its own Representative in Congress.

Mandaluyong at the turn of the century was proclaimed by the city's grand dads as the Millennium City, having come a long way from being a forested rolling hill to a bustling city of vibrant economic activities. It was recently named the new tiger city of Metro Manila, among other accomplishments. Mandaluyong today is composed of 27 barangays divided into two political districts mainly by Boni Avenue and G. Aglipay Street. As of January 9, 2002, it has 1,238 voting precincts and a total of 166,037 registered voters.

Synthesis

The results of the 2016 national elections highlighted the dominance of political dynasties in the country. Despite overwhelming recognition that political dynasties breed patronage politics and corruption, no substantial steps have been undertaken to address this issue. The review here examines the general nature of Philippine political dynasties, the reasons for their continuing existence and their adverse impact on the country. There are probably problem that emanates and basically this could come from three factors: (1) the political and socio-economic foundations upon which political dynasties are built; 2) the inability to effectively implement Philippine constitutional provisions by enacting an enabling law; and 3) the weakness of potential countervailing forces that would challenge political dynasties.

3
RESEARCH METHODOLOGY

This chapter discusses the methods of research used, population frame and sampling description of the respondent, data gathering procedure, instruments used and data analysis.

Research Method Used

This study made use of the descriptive quantitative research with a survey of the respondents and further analysis of documents gathered through the response of the respondents being surveyed about their perception on the political dynasty in Mandaluyong City.

Population Frame and Sampling Scheme

The population of the study is supposed to be composed of five hundred (500) respondents, who are also registered voters from twenty-five (25) barangays of Mandaluyong City. The researchers surveyed five hundred (500) registered voters of these and each was given survey questionnaires to get his perspective on the said study.

Description of the Respondents

The respondents of the study were five hundred (500) registered voters from twenty-five (25) barangays of Mandaluyong City. Respondents were stratified into men and women, aged eighteen (18) years and above. The researchers also asked the educational attainment and monthly income of the respondents. The researchers believed that these persons were appropriate subjects of this study from which they provide an adequate data to supply all the information needed.

Instrument

A survey questionnaire was given to the residents of each selected barangay to answer questions that are related to the objective of the study. Each survey questionnaire had twenty-eight (28) questions to support the objectives of the study. The questionnaire was divided into four (4) parts: reasons, positive effects, negative effects, and strategies.

Data Gathering Procedure

The researchers asked the Election Officer of Commission on Elections - Mandaluyong City of the official number of registered voters of each barangays. The researchers have presented letters, to the election officer, noted by the thesis adviser and thesis professor for the validity of the research study. As the Election Officer handed the list of registered voters, the researchers started conducting the survey. The researchers also asked permission from Chairpersons of respective barangays. Initially, the researchers wished to conduct survey in all twenty-seven (27) barangays of Mandaluyong City. Unfortunately, Barangay Barangka Itaas & Barangay Wack-Wack could not accommodate the researchers. Thus, the latter reduced the respondents from five hundred forty (540) to five hundred (500) participants. The respondents from twenty-five (25) barangays were five hundred (500) registered voters. The survey questionnaires had twenty (28) suitable questions that fit the objectives of the study.

The researchers assured the confidentiality of the survey sheets. The researchers gave the respondent an option of being anonymous before answering the survey questionnaire.

Statistical Treatment

Descriptive statistics was used to interpret the demographic profile and data gathered from the perception of the respondents towards political dynasty through survey questionnaire.

Specifically, the descriptive statistics such as the frequency counts that were transmuted to percentage were used to present the data on the profile of the voters of Mandaluyong city.

Likert scale
Figure 4

Scale	Weighted Mean	Verbal Interpretation
5	4.50-5.00	Strongly Agree (SD)
4	3.50-4.49	Agree (A)
3	2.50-3.49	Neutral (N)
2	1.50-2.49	Disagree (D)
1	1.00-1.49	Strongly Disagree (SD)

Weighted Mean (WM). It was utilized to determine the interpretation in every question.
Formula:

$$M = \frac{\Sigma f x}{N}$$

Where:
  M= Weighted Mean
  Σ= Summation of
  f= Frequency
  x= Weight given to the respondents
  N= Sample

Percentage. It was used to test to show the proposition of the respondents with respect to their profiles and variables.
Formula:

$$P = \frac{f}{N} \times 100$$

Where:
  P= Percentage
  n= Sample
  N= total level of respondents

4
PRESENTATION, ANALYSIS AND INTERPRETATION OF DATA

This chapter includes the presentation, analysis, and interpretation of data gathered from the respondents in order to answer specific problems.

The purpose of the study is to determine if there is a significant difference on the perceived effects and reasons of the existence of Political Dynasty by profile.

1. Demographic Profile of the Respondents

Table 1
Distribution of Respondents According to Age

AGE	FREQUENCY	PERCENTAGE
18-35 years old	249	49.8%
36-45 years old	118	23.6%
46-above	133	26.6%
TOTAL	500	100%

Table 1 shows the total number and percentage distribution of respondents according to age

From a total of 500 participants, 49.8% or 249 were under age ranging from 18-35 years old, and 26.6% and 23.6% respectively, belong to ages 36-45 and 46 and above. Basically, majority of the respondents belong to ages 18-35 years old.

Table 2
Distribution of Respondents According to Gender

GENDER	FREQUENCY	PERCENTAGE
Male	211	42.2%
Female	289	57.8%
TOTAL	500	100%

Table 2 shows the distribution of respondents according to their gender

It can be seen that the male respondents had a frequency of 211 or an equivalent of 42.2% and the female respondents had a frequency of 289 or an equivalent of 57.8%. Basically, female respondents prevail in this research than the male respondents.

Table 3
Distribution of Respondents According to Monthly Income

MONTHLY INCOME	FREQUENCY	PERCENTAGE
10,000-below	238	47.6%
11,000-20,000	233	46.6%
21,000-above	29	5.8%
TOTAL	500	100%

Table 3 shows the distribution of respondents according to monthly income

It can be seen that respondents with monthly income of 10,000 and below had a frequency of 238 or an equivalent of 47.6%. Respondents with monthly income of 11,000 to 20,000 had a frequency of 233 or an equivalent of 46.6%. Lastly, respondents with monthly income of 21,000 and above had a frequency of 29 or an equivalent of 5.8%. With this, it shows that majority of the respondents had a monthly income of 10,000 and below.

Table 4
Reasons of Existence of Political Dynasty According to Aged 18-35 Years old

INDICATORS	WEIGHTED MEAN	VERBAL INTERPRETATION
Political dynasty exists because of gratitude.	3.87	AGREE
Political dynasty exists because of money as used for political machinery.	3.82	AGREE
Members of a political family are popular because they reign for a long period of time.	4.24	AGREE
Voters trust political families because they are proven and tested by time.	3.91	AGREE
Political dynasty exists because voters have inadequate knowledge of the candidates.	3.67	AGREE
People have poor judgment in selecting officials.	3.56	AGREE
Most of the running candidates came from a political family.	4	AGREE
Voters believe that these political families are more knowledgeable because of their background and experiences.	3.81	AGREE
Some candidates came from wealthy and powerful families.	3.30	NEUTRAL
The voters believe that these politicians could help them in exchange of their votes.	3.90	AGREE
OVERALL WEIGHTED MEAN	3.81	AGREE

Table 4 shows the reasons of existence of Political Dynasty for respondents aged 18-35 years old

Item number 3 states that *"Members of a political family are popular because they reign for a long period of time"* got the highest weighted mean value of 4.24 on which the verbal interpretation is Agree. However, the item number 9 that states *"Some candidates came from wealthy and powerful families"* got the lowest weighted mean value of 3.30 on which the verbal interpretation is Neutral. This table for age 18-35 years old got an overall weighted mean value of 3.81 on which the verbal interpretation is Agree. The table shows that the over all selected is agree. It illustrates that 18-35 years old are more exposed in social media like radio and television which affects them to agree on this questions.

Table 5
Positive Effects of Political Dynasty According to Aged 18-35 Years Old

INDICATORS	WEIGHTED MEAN	VERBAL INTERPRETATION
Political dynasties provide political stability.	3.69	AGREE
Administration of these political families were tested and proven by time.	3.80	AGREE
Members of a political family know their job more than others because of their experiences in politics.	3.59	AGREE
These politicians provide good economic performance.	3.69	AGREE
Long-term programs can be met with the help of political dynasties because there is no transmission of political power.	3.76	AGREE
Political dynasty hones an aspiring leader from a political family because children belonging in political families are being trained by their kin.	3.83	AGREE
OVERALL WEIGHTED MEAN	3.73	AGREE

Table 5 shows the positive effects of Political Dynasty for respondents aged 18-35 years old

Item number 6 states that *"Political dynasty hones an aspiring leader from a political family because children belonging in political families are being trained by their kin"* got the highest weighted mean value of 3.83 on which the verbal interpretation is Agree. While, item number 3 that states *"Members of a political family know their job more than others because of their experiences in politics"* got the lowest weighted mean value of 3.59 on which the verbal interpretation is Agree. Table 5 disclosed the positive effects of Political

Dynasty for respondents aged 18-35 years old. As revealed by the table, the overall weighted mean value of the positive effects of Political Dynasty for respondents aged 18-35 years old is 3.73 on which the verbal interpretation is Agree.

This age bracket believes that political dynasty is beneficial on which political family tends to have proper background on politics and is most likely to be well-versed when it comes to politics. They would know what to do and they would know how to work with problems because they have probably learned it already from their relatives. Knowing what to do when leading people is a huge factor and this actually helps in becoming a great leader. It also illustrates that even if people choose the same officials, there are positive effects like the continuity of projects. People also wanted a continuation of projects which benefit them.

Table 6
Negative Effects of Political Dynasty According to Aged 18-35 Years Old

INDICATORS	WEIGHTED MEAN	VERBAL INTERPRETATION
Corruption is always present.	4.37	AGREE
A political family can be a tyrant because of the power it holds.	4.07	AGREE
Political dynasties promote dirty politics because of self-serving interests.	3.83	AGREE
Political dynasty can undermine the quality of democracy by means of limiting the chances of non-dynastic to run in a position.	3.88	AGREE
Rural areas with a high level of political dynasties display a higher level of poverty.	3.73	AGREE
Political dynasty limits the chances of ordinary but qualified Filipinos	3.95	AGREE
OVERALL WEIGHTED MEAN	3.97	AGREE

Table 6 shows the negative effects of Political Dynasty for respondents aged 18-35 years old

Item number 1 states that *"Corruption is always present"* got the highest weighted mean value of 4.37 which the verbal interpretation is Agree. While, the item number 5 that states *"Rural areas with a high level of political dynasties display a higher level of poverty"* got the lowest weighted mean value of 3.73 which the verbal interpretation is Agree. The overall weighted mean value of the negative effects of Political Dynasty for respondents aged 18-35 years old is 3.97 which the verbal interpretation is Agree.

It is revealed here the negative connotations that corrupt officials may give opportunity to allow their relatives who may also be influenced by them and turn out to be corrupt as well. Aside from that, some people think that political dynasty can cause corruption. 18-30 years old is most exposed to the political status of the country. Age 18-30 years old have a job which means that this age is on working status.

Table 7
Strategies to Regulate Political Dynasty According to Aged 18-35 Years Old

INDICATORS	WEIGHTED MEAN	VERBAL INTERPRETATION
The Congress must define political dynasty and its content by passing the Anti-Political Dynasty Bill.	4.13	AGREE
Citizens must attend voting seminars.	4.27	AGREE
Educate people to vote more responsibly in choosing a leader.	4.25	AGREE
Limit the family members that are running for the government position.	4.11	AGREE
Concentrate on information campaign in support of non-dynastic candidates in media.	4.06	AGREE
All universities must include politics and government in their curriculum.	4.31	AGREE
OVERALL WEIGHTED MEAN	4.19	AGREE

Table 7 shows strategies to regulate Political Dynasty for respondents aged 18-35 years old

Item number 6 states that "*All universities must include politics and government in their curriculum*" got the highest weighted mean value of 4.31 which the verbal interpretation is Agree. However, the item number 5 that states "*Concentrate on information campaign in support of non-dynastic candidates in media*" got the lowest weighted mean value of 4.06 which the verbal interpretation is Agree.

The overall weighted mean value of the strategies to regulate Political Dynasty for respondents aged 18-35 years old is 4.19 which the verbal interpretation is Agree. On the light of personal belief, the respondents agreed about limiting dynasties and the dangers posed by it to the task of development and good governance. It can be said that not only limit voters' options but also hinder cities and provinces from reaching their full potential.

Table 8
Reasons of Existence of Political Dynasty According to Aged 36-45 Years Old

INDICATORS	WEIGHTED MEAN	VERBAL INTERPRETATION
Political dynasty exists because of gratitude.	4.07	AGREE
Political dynasty exists because of money as used for political machinery.	4.18	AGREE
Members of a political family are popular because they reign for a long period of time.	4.42	AGREE
Voters trust political families because they are proven and tested by time.	4.13	AGREE
Political dynasty exists because voters have inadequate knowledge of the candidates.	3.64	AGREE
People have poor judgment in selecting officials.	3.64	AGREE
Most of the running candidates came from a political family.	4.21	AGREE
Voters believe that these political families are more knowledgeable because of their background and experiences.	3.92	AGREE
Some candidates came from wealthy and powerful families.	4.18	AGREE
The voters believe that these politicians could help them in exchange of their votes.	3.83	AGREE
OVERALL WEIGHTED MEAN	4.02	AGREE

Table 8 shows the reasons of existence of Political Dynasty for respondents aged 36-45 years old

Item number 3 states that "*Members of a political family are popular because they reign for a long period of time*" got the highest weighted mean value of 4.42 which the verbal interpretation is Agree. While, items numbers 5 and 6 that states "*Political dynasty exists because voters have inadequate knowledge of the candidates*" and "People have poor judgment in selecting officials", respectively, got the lowest weighted mean value of 3.64 which the verbal interpretation is Agree.

The overall weighted mean value of reasons of existence of Political Dynasty for respondents aged 36-45 years old is 4.02 which the verbal interpretation is Agree. For item number 3, the this table for this age bracket here has got the same high result with age bracket of 18-35 on which it speaks of political dynasties provide strong and capable leaders, well-known and respected in their regions and the name that they hear most of the time.

Table 9
Positive Effects of Political Dynasty According to Aged 36 to 45 Years Old

INDICATORS	WEIGHTED MEAN	VERBAL INTERPRETATION
Political dynasties provide political stability.	3.57	AGREE
Administration of these political families were tested and proven by time.	3.90	AGREE
Members of a political family know their job more than others because of their experiences in politics.	3.82	AGREE
These politicians provide good economic performance.	3.65	AGREE
Long-term programs can be met with the help of political dynasties because there is no transmission of political power.	3.68	AGREE
Political dynasty hones an aspiring leader from a political family because children belonging in political families are being trained by their kin.	3.97	AGREE
OVERALL WEIGHTED MEAN	3.77	AGREE

Table 9 shows the positive effects of Political Dynasty for respondents aged 36-45 years old

Item number 6 states that "*Political dynasty hones an aspiring leader from a political family because children belonging in political families are being trained by their kin*" got the highest weighted mean value of 3.97 which the verbal interpretation is Agree. While, item number 1 that states "*Political dynasties provide political stability*" got the lowest weighted mean value of 3.57 which the verbal interpretation is Agree.

The overall weighted mean value of positive effects of Political Dynasty for respondents aged 36-45 years old is 3.77 which the verbal interpretation is Agree. Both age bracket of 18-35 and 36-45 agreed that the future is uncertain if it is either good seed or bad seed. Somehow, a good leader if not made then it is moulded. If an individual is born with parents who are good politicians, there is a potential he will be a good leader himself.

Table 10
Negative Effects of Political Dynasty According to Aged 36 to 45 Years Old

INDICATORS	WEIGHTED MEAN	VERBAL INTERPRETATION
Corruption is always present.	4.46	AGREE
A political family can be a tyrant because of the power it holds.	4.10	AGREE
Political dynasties promote dirty politics because of self-serving interests.	4.08	AGREE
Political dynasty can undermine the quality of democracy by means of limiting the chances of non-dynastic to run in a position.	3.97	AGREE
Rural areas with a high level of political dynasties display a higher level of poverty.	3.81	AGREE
Political dynasty limits the chances of ordinary but qualified Filipinos	3.96	AGREE
OVERALL WEIGHTED MEAN	4.06	AGREE

Table 10 shows the negative effects of Political Dynasty for respondents aged 36-45 years old

Item number 1 states that *"Corruption is always present"* got the highest weighted mean value of 4.46 which the verbal interpretation is Agree. However, item number 5 that states *"Rural areas with a high level of political dynasties display a higher level of poverty"* got the lowest weighted mean value of 3.81 which the verbal interpretation is Agree.

The overall weighted mean value of negative effects of Political Dynasty for respondents aged 36-45 years old is 4.06 which the verbal interpretation is Agree. The same result with the previous age bracket, respondents age 36-45 believes that families protect each other, therefore protects corrupt practices. As in business monopolies, politics are very dangerous and detrimental in society. Genuine opposition should always be present as there are always at least two sides to one coin.

Table 11
Strategies to Regulate Political Dynasty According to Aged 36 to 45 Years Old

INDICATORS	WEIGHTED MEAN	VERBAL INTERPRETATION
The Congress must define political dynasty and its content by passing the Anti-Political Dynasty Bill.	4.21	AGREE
Citizens must attend voting seminars.	4.40	AGREE
Educate people to vote more responsibly in choosing a leader.	4.29	AGREE
Limit the family members that are running for the government position.	4.30	AGREE
Concentrate on information campaign in support of non-dynastic candidates in media.	4.30	AGREE
All universities must include politics and government in their curriculum.	4.39	AGREE
OVERALL WEIGHTED MEAN	4.32	AGREE

Table 11 shows the strategies to regulate Political Dynasty for respondents aged 36-45 years old

Item number 6 states that "*All universities must include politics and government in their curriculum.*" got the highest weighted mean value of 4.39 which the verbal interpretation is Agree. While, item number 1 that states "*The Congress must define political dynasty and its content by passing the Anti-Dynasty Bill.*" got the lowest weighted mean value of 4.21 which the verbal interpretation is Agree. The overall weighted mean value of strategies to regulate Political Dynasty for respondents aged 36-45 years old is 4.32 which the verbal interpretation is Agree.

This table also discloses that awareness through education must be included in the curriculum since the historic character of electoral politics in the Philippines has an impact in its socio-economic state. It illustrates that people age 18-30 believes that political dynasty will regulate. It depends on people if they vote the same officials again.

Table 12
Reasons of Existence of Political Dynasty According to Aged 46 Years Old and above

INDICATORS	WEIGHTED MEAN	VERBAL INTERPRETATION
Political dynasty exists because of gratitude.	3.76	AGREE
Political dynasty exists because of money as used for political machinery.	3.98	AGREE
Members of a political family are popular because they reign for a long period of time.	4.11	AGREE
Voters trust political families because they are proven and tested by time.	3.98	AGREE
Political dynasty exists because voters have inadequate knowledge of the candidates.	3.54	AGREE
People have poor judgment in selecting officials.	3.62	AGREE
Most of the running candidates came from a political family.	3.98	AGREE
Voters believe that these political families are more knowledgeable because of their background and experiences.	3.90	AGREE
Some candidates came from wealthy and powerful families.	3.96	AGREE
The voters believe that these politicians could help them in exchange of their votes.	3.74	AGREE
OVERALL WEIGHTED MEAN	3.86	AGREE

Table 12 shows the reasons of existence of Political Dynasty for respondents aged 46 years old and above

Item number 3 states that "*Members of a political family are popular because they reign for a long period of time*" got the highest weighted mean value of 4.11 which the verbal interpretation is Agree. While, item number 5 that states "*Political dynasty exists because voters have inadequate knowledge of the candidates*" got the lowest weighted mean value of 3.54 which the verbal interpretation is Agree.

The overall weighted mean value of reasons of existence of Political Dynasty for respondents aged 46 years old and above is 3.86 which the verbal interpretation is Agree. Along with other age brackets, this table discloses the abuse of political dynasty to our weak democratic structures on how relatives of previous incumbents exclusively benefit from the political investments of their predecessors which, in turn, consolidates disproportionate political power in a few families. People age 40 and above illustrates that they agreed on this perceptions of political dynasty.

Table 13
Positive Effects of Political Dynasty According to Aged 46 Years Old and Above

INDICATORS	WEIGHTED MEAN	VERBAL INTERPRETATION
Political dynasties provide political stability.	3.56	AGREE
Administration of these political families were tested and proven by time.	3.78	AGREE
Members of a political family know their job more than others because of their experiences in politics.	3.75	AGREE
These politicians provide good economic performance.	3.60	AGREE
Long-term programs can be met with the help of political dynasties because there is no transmission of political power.	3.77	AGREE
Political dynasty hones an aspiring leader from a political family because children belonging in political families are being trained by their kin.	3.98	AGREE
OVERALL WEIGHTED MEAN	3.74	AGREE

Table 13 shows the positive effects of Political Dynasty for respondents aged 46 years old and above

Item number 6 states that "*Political dynasty hones an aspiring leader from a political family because children belonging in political families are being trained by their kin*" got the highest weighted mean value of 3.98 which the verbal interpretation is Agree. While, item number 1 that states "*Political dynasties provide political stability*" got the lowest weighted mean value of 3.56 which the verbal interpretation is Agree.

The overall weighted mean value of positive effects of Political Dynasty for respondents aged 46 years old and above is 3.74 which the verbal interpretation is Agree. Likewise, this table for this age bracket agrees that elections have formalized the process of political succession through a periodic democratic exercise which can be easily manipulated for selfish ends.

Elite rule is legitimized through this process by giving the illusion that the public has the power to choose its leaders, even though the pool of electable candidates is generally limited to a set of individuals with familiar surnames whose been honed and trained to become one. A person age 40 and above, says that political dynasty also has positive effects in society. They both agreed that political dynasty can help the society too.

Table 14
Negative Effects of Political Dynasty According to
Aged 46 Years Old and Above

INDICATORS	WEIGHTED MEAN	VERBAL INTERPRETATION
Corruption is always present.	4.23	AGREE
A political family can be a tyrant because of the power it holds.	4.10	AGREE
Political dynasties promote dirty politics because of self-serving interests.	3.93	AGREE
Political dynasty can undermine the quality of democracy by means of limiting the chances of non-dynastic to run in a position.	3.95	AGREE
Rural areas with a high level of political dynasties display a higher level of poverty.	3.81	AGREE
Political dynasty limits the chances of ordinary but qualified Filipinos	4.07	AGREE
OVERALL WEIGHTED MEAN	4.02	AGREE

Table 14 shows the negative effects of Political Dynasty for respondents aged 46 years old and above

Item number 1 states that "*Corruption is always present*" got the highest weighted mean value of 4.23 which the verbal interpretation is Agree. However, item number 5 that states "*Rural areas with a higher level of political dynasties display a higher level of poverty*" got the lowest weighted mean value of 3.81 which the verbal interpretation is Agree.

The overall weighted mean value of negative effects of Political Dynasty for respondents aged 46 years old and above is 4.02 which the verbal interpretation is Agree. Similarly, these age brackets believe that political power is closely linked to economic power. This table shows that most people stick on the negative sides of political dynasty.

Table 15
Strategies to Regulate Political Dynasty According to Aged 46 Years Old And Above

INDICATORS	WEIGHTED MEAN	VERBAL INTERPRETATION
The Congress must define political dynasty and its content by passing the Anti-Political Dynasty Bill.	4.17	AGREE
Citizens must attend voting seminars.	4.32	AGREE
Educate people to vote more responsibly in choosing a leader.	4.26	AGREE
Limit the family members that are running for the government position.	4.29	AGREE
Concentrate on information campaign in support of non-dynastic candidates in media.	4.20	AGREE
All universities must include politics and government in their curriculum.	4.36	AGREE
OVERALL WEIGHTED MEAN	4.27	AGREE

Table 15 shows the strategies to regulate Political Dynasty for respondents aged 46 years old and above

Item number 6 states that "All universities must include politics and government in their curriculum" got the highest weighted mean value of 4.36 which the verbal interpretation is Agree. While, item number 1 that states "The Congress must define political dynasty and its content by passing the Anti-Dynasty Bill" got the lowest weighted mean value of 4.17 which the verbal interpretation is Agree. The overall weighted mean value of strategies to regulate Political Dynasty for respondents aged 46 years old and above is 4.27 which the verbal interpretation is Agree.

Furthermore, this table shows that respondents approve if there will be any ardent effort to advance the need for including political dynasty in education. It shows that these strategies will help to lessen the political dynasty.

Table 16
Reasons of Existence of Political Dynasty According to Female

INDICATORS	WEIGHTED MEAN	VERBAL INTERPRETATION
Political dynasty exists because of gratitude.	3.79	AGREE
Political dynasty exists because of money as used for political machinery.	3.81	AGREE
Members of a political family are popular because they reign for a long period of time.	4.21	AGREE
Voters trust political families because they are proven and tested by time.	4.03	AGREE
Political dynasty exists because voters have inadequate knowledge of the candidates.	3.56	AGREE
People have poor judgment in selecting officials.	3.58	AGREE
Most of the running candidates came from a political family.	4.03	AGREE
Voters believe that these political families are more knowledgeable because of their background and experiences.	3.85	AGREE
Some candidates came from wealthy and powerful families.	4.07	AGREE
The voters believe that these politicians could help them in exchange of their votes.	3.83	AGREE
OVERALL WEIGHTED MEAN	3.88	AGREE

Table 16 shows the reasons of existence of Political Dynasty for female respondents.

Item number 3 states that "*Members of a political family are popular because they reign for a long period of time*" got the highest weighted mean value of 4.21 which the verbal interpretation is Agree. While, item number 5 that states "*Political dynasty exists because voters have inadequate knowledge of the candidates*" got the lowest weighted mean value of 3.56 which the verbal interpretation is Agree.

The overall weighted mean value of reasons of existence of Political Dynasty for female respondents is 3.88 which the verbal interpretation is Agree. It only shows that female believes that dynasty exist because some of the candidates are not known that it results to choosing or voting to the popular candidate.

Table 17
Positive Effects of Political Dynasty According to Female

INDICATORS	WEIGHTED MEAN	VERBAL INTERPRETATION
Political dynasties provide political stability.	3.66	AGREE
Administration of these political families were tested and proven by time.	3.81	AGREE
Members of a political family know their job more than others because of their experiences in politics.	3.68	AGREE
These politicians provide good economic performance.	3.72	AGREE
Long-term programs can be met with the help of political dynasties because there is no transmission of political power.	3.75	AGREE
Political dynasty hones an aspiring leader from a political family because children belonging in political families are being trained by their kin.	3.90	AGREE
OVERALL WEIGHTED MEAN	3.75	AGREE

Table 17 shows the positive effects of Political Dynasty for female respondents

Item number 6 states that "*Political dynasty hones an aspiring leader from a political family because children belonging in political families are being trained by their kin*" got the highest weighted mean value of 3.90 which the verbal interpretation is Agree. While, item number 1 that states "*Political dynasties provide political stability.*" got the lowest weighted mean value of 3.66 which the verbal interpretation is Agree.

The overall weighted mean value of positive effects of Political Dynasty for female respondents is 3.75 which the verbal interpretation is Agree. Female voter agrees to all the positive effects that is given in the survey questionnaire, a good leader are trained by those leader who have experienced.

Table 18
Negative Effects of Political Dynasty According to Female

INDICATORS	WEIGHTED MEAN	VERBAL INTERPRETATION
Corruption is always present.	4.29	AGREE
A political family can be a tyrant because of the power it holds.	4.01	AGREE
Political dynasties promote dirty politics because of self-serving interests.	3.99	AGREE
Political dynasty can undermine the quality of democracy by means of limiting the chances of non-dynastic to run in a position.	3.92	AGREE
Rural areas with a high level of political dynasties display a higher level of poverty.	3.83	AGREE
Political dynasty limits the chances of ordinary but qualified Filipinos	4.03	AGREE
OVERALL WEIGHTED MEAN	4.01	AGREE

Table 18 shows the negative effect of Political Dynasty for female respondents

Item number 1 states that "*Corruption is always present.*" got the highest weighted mean value of 4.29 which the verbal interpretation is Agree. Item number 5 that states "*Rural areas with a high level of political dynasties display a higher level of poverty.*" got the lowest weighted mean value of 3.83 which the verbal interpretation is Agree.

The overall weighted mean value of negative effects of Political Dynasty for female respondents is 4.01 which the verbal interpretation is Agree. Female still agrees to the statement of number 5 that rural areas with a high level of political dynasties display a higher level of poverty because they believe that in political dynasty corruption is always present.

Table 19
Strategies to Regulate Political Dynasty According to Female

INDICATORS	WEIGHTED MEAN	VERBAL INTERPRETATION
The Congress must define political dynasty and its content by passing the Anti-Political Dynasty Bill.	4.23	AGREE
Citizens must attend voting seminars.	4.37	AGREE
Educate people to vote more responsibly in choosing a leader.	4.35	AGREE
Limit the family members that are running for the government position.	4.21	AGREE
Concentrate on information campaign in support of non-dynastic candidates in media.	4.11	AGREE
All universities must include politics and government in their curriculum.	4.31	AGREE
OVERALL WEIGHTED MEAN	4.27	AGREE

Table 19 shows the strategies to regulate Political Dynasty for female respondents

Item number 2 states that "*Citizens must attend voting seminars*" got the highest weighted mean value of 4.37 which the verbal interpretation is Agree. While, item number 5 that states "*Concentrate on information campaign in support of non-dynastic candidates in media*" got the lowest weighted mean value of 4.11 which the verbal interpretation is Agree.

The overall weighted mean value of strategies to regulate Political Dynasty for female respondents is 4.27 which the verbal interpretation is Agree.

Table 20
Reasons of Existence of Political Dynasty According to Male

INDICATORS	WEIGHTED MEAN	VERBAL INTERPRETATION
Political dynasty exists because of gratitude.	4	AGREE
Political dynasty exists because of money as used for political machinery.	4.02	AGREE
Members of a political family are popular because they reign for a long period of time.	4.34	AGREE
Voters trust political families because they are proven and tested by time.	3.90	AGREE
Political dynasty exists because voters have inadequate knowledge of the candidates.	3.70	AGREE
People have poor judgment in selecting officials.	3.63	AGREE
Most of the running candidates came from a political family.	4.08	AGREE
Voters believe that these political families are more knowledgeable because of their background and experiences.	3.87	AGREE
Some candidates came from wealthy and powerful families.	4.04	AGREE
The voters believe that these politicians could help them in exchange of their votes.	3.94	AGREE
OVERALL WEIGHTED MEAN	3.95	AGREE

Table 20 shows the reasons of existence of Political Dynasty for male respondents

Item number 3 states that "*Members of a political family are popular because they reign for a long period of time.*" got the highest weighted mean value of 4.34 which the verbal interpretation is Agree. While, item number 6 that states "*People have poor judgment in selecting officials.*" got the lowest weighted mean value of 3.63 which the verbal interpretation is Agree.

The overall weighted mean value of reasons of existence of Political Dynasty for male respondents is 3.95 which the verbal interpretation is Agree.

Table 21
Positive Effects of Political Dynasty According to Male

INDICATORS	WEIGHTED MEAN	VERBAL INTERPRETATION
Political dynasties provide political stability.	3.35	NEUTRAL
Administration of these political families were tested and proven by time.	3.83	AGREE
Members of a political family know their job more than others because of their experiences in politics.	3.70	AGREE
These politicians provide good economic performance.	3.61	AGREE
Long-term programs can be met with the help of political dynasties because there is no transmission of political power.	3.78	AGREE
Political dynasty hones an aspiring leader from a political family because children belonging in political families are being trained by their kin.	3.52	AGREE
OVERALL WEIGHTED MEAN	3.63	AGREE

Table 21 shows the positive effects of Political Dynasty for male respondents

Item number 2 states that "*Administration of these political families were tested and proven by time.*" got the highest weighted mean value of 3.83 which the verbal interpretation is Agree. While, item number 1 that states "*Political dynasties provide political stability.*" got the lowest weighted mean value of 3.35 which the verbal interpretation is Neutral.

The overall weighted mean value of positive effects of Political Dynasty for male respondents is 3.63 which the verbal interpretation is Agree.

Table 22
Negative Effects of Political Dynasty According to Male

INDICATORS	WEIGHTED MEAN	VERBAL INTERPRETATION
Corruption is always present.	4.36	AGREE
A political family can be a tyrant because of the power it holds.	4.19	AGREE
Political dynasties promote dirty politics because of self-serving interests.	3.86	AGREE
Political dynasty can undermine the quality of democracy by means of limiting the chances of non-dynastic to run in a position.	3.94	AGREE
Rural areas with a high level of political dynasties display a higher level of poverty.	3.81	AGREE
Political dynasty limits the chances of ordinary but qualified Filipinos	4	AGREE
OVERALL WEIGHTED MEAN	4.03	AGREE

Table 22 shows the negative effects of Political Dynasty for male respondents

Item number 1 states that *"Corruption is always present."* got the highest weighted mean value of 4.36 which the verbal interpretation is Agree. Item number 5 that states *"Rural areas with a high level of political dynasties display a higher level of poverty."* got the lowest weighted mean value of 3.81 which the verbal interpretation is Agree. The overall weighted mean value of negative effects of Political Dynasty for male respondents is 4.03 which the verbal interpretation is Agree.

Table 23
Strategies to Regulate Political Dynasty According to Male

INDICATORS	WEIGHTED MEAN	VERBAL INTERPRETATION
The Congress must define political dynasty and its content by passing the Anti-Political Dynasty Bill.	4.10	AGREE
Citizens must attend voting seminars.	4.22	AGREE
Educate people to vote more responsibly in choosing a leader.	4.15	AGREE
Limit the family members that are running for the government position.	4.18	AGREE
Concentrate on information campaign in support of non-dynastic candidates in media.	4.17	AGREE
All universities must include politics and government in their curriculum.	4.33	AGREE
OVERALL WEIGHTED MEAN	4.19	AGREE

Table 23 shows the strategies to regulate Political Dynasty for male respondents

Item number 6 states that "*All universities must include politics and government in their curriculum.*" got the highest weighted mean value of 4.33 which the verbal interpretation is Agree. While, item number 1 that states "*The Congress must define political dynasty and its content by passing the Anti-Dynasty Bill.*" got the lowest weighted mean value of 4.10 which the verbal interpretation is Agree.

The overall weighted mean value of strategies to regulate Political Dynasty for male respondents is 4.19 which the verbal interpretation is Agree.

Table 24
Reasons of Existence of Political Dynasty According to Monthly Income of 10,000 and Below

INDICATORS	WEIGHTED MEAN	VERBAL INTERPRETATION
Political dynasty exists because of gratitude.	3.56	AGREE
Political dynasty exists because of money as used for political machinery.	3.76	AGREE
Members of a political family are popular because they reign for a long period of time.	3.56	AGREE
Voters trust political families because they are proven and tested by time.	3.98	AGREE
Political dynasty exists because voters have inadequate knowledge of the candidates.	3.59	AGREE
People have poor judgment in selecting officials.	3.57	AGREE
Most of the running candidates came from a political family.	3.94	AGREE
Voters believe that these political families are more knowledgeable because of their background and experiences.	3.97	AGREE
Some candidates came from wealthy and powerful families.	3.89	AGREE
The voters believe that these politicians could help them in exchange of their votes.	3.86	AGREE
OVERALL WEIGHTED MEAN	3.77	AGREE

Table 24 shows the reasons of existence of Political Dynasty for respondents with monthly income of 10,000 and below

Item number 8 states that "*Voters believe that these political families are more knowledgeable because of their background and experiences.*" got the highest weighted mean value of 3.97 which the verbal interpretation is Agree. However, items numbers 1 and 3 that states "*Political dynasty exists because of gratitude.*" and "Members of a political family are popular because they reign for a long period of time.", respectively, got the lowest weighted mean value of 3.56 which the verbal interpretation is Agree.

The overall weighted mean value of reasons of existence of Political Dynasty for respondents with monthly income of 10,000 and below is 3.90 which the verbal interpretation is Agree.

Table 25
Positive Effects of Political Dynasty According to Monthly Income of 10,000 and Below

INDICATORS	WEIGHTED MEAN	VERBAL INTERPRETATION
Political dynasties provide political stability.	3.56	AGREE
Administration of these political families were tested and proven by time.	3.83	AGREE
Members of a political family know their job more than others because of their experiences in politics.	3.80	AGREE
These politicians provide good economic performance.	3.83	AGREE
Long-term programs can be met with the help of political dynasties because there is no transmission of political power.	3.80	AGREE
Political dynasty hones an aspiring leader from a political family because children belonging in political families are being trained by their kin.	3.87	AGREE
OVERALL WEIGHTED MEAN	3.78	AGREE

Table 25 shows the positive effects of Political Dynasty for respondents with monthly income of 10,000 and below

Item number 6 that states "*Political dynasty hones an aspiring leader from a political family because children belonging in political families are being trained by their kin.*" got the highest weighted mean value of 3.87 which the verbal interpretation is Agree. However, item number 1 that states "*Political dynasties provide political stability.*" got the lowest weighted mean value of 3.56 which the verbal interpretation is Agree.

The overall weighted mean value of positive effects of Political Dynasty for respondents with monthly income of 10,000 and below is 3.78 which the verbal interpretation is Agree.

Table 26
Negative Effects of Political Dynasty According to Monthly Income of 10,000 and Below

INDICATORS	WEIGHTED MEAN	VERBAL INTERPRETATION
Corruption is always present.	4.21	AGREE
A political family can be a tyrant because of the power it holds.	3.98	AGREE
Political dynasties promote dirty politics because of self-serving interests.	3.88	AGREE
Political dynasty can undermine the quality of democracy by means of limiting the chances of non-dynastic to run in a position.	3.90	AGREE
Rural areas with a high level of political dynasties display a higher level of poverty.	3.81	AGREE
Political dynasty limits the chances of ordinary but qualified Filipinos	3.68	AGREE
OVERALL WEIGHTED MEAN	3.91	AGREE

Table 26 shows the negative effects of Political Dynasty for respondents with monthly income of 10,000 and below.

Item number 1 states that "*Corruption is always present.*" got the highest weighted mean value of 4.21 which the verbal interpretation is Agree. However, item number 5 that states "*Rural areas with a high level of political dynasties display a higher level of poverty.*" got the lowest weighted mean value of 3.68 which the verbal interpretation is Agree.

The overall weighted mean value of negative effects of Political Dynasty for respondents with monthly income of 10,000 and below is 3.91 which the verbal interpretation is Agree.

Table 27
Strategies to Regulate Political Dynasty According to Monthly Income of 10,000 and Below

INDICATORS	WEIGHTED MEAN	VERBAL INTERPRETATION
The Congress must define political dynasty and its content by passing the Anti-Political Dynasty Bill.	3.58	AGREE
Citizens must attend voting seminars.	4.26	AGREE
Educate people to vote more responsibly in choosing a leader.	4.36	AGREE
Limit the family members that are running for the government position.	4.08	AGREE
Concentrate on information campaign in support of non-dynastic candidates in media.	4.08	AGREE
All universities must include politics and government in their curriculum.	4.22	AGREE
OVERALL WEIGHTED MEAN	4.09	AGREE

Table 27 shows the strategies to regulate Political Dynasty for respondents with monthly income of 10,000 and below

Item number 3 states that *"Educate people to vote more responsibly in choosing a leader."* got the highest weighted mean value of 4.36 which the verbal interpretation is Agree. However, item number 1 that states *"The Congress must define political dynasty and its content by passing the Anti-Dynasty Bill."* got the lowest weighted mean value of 3.58 which the verbal interpretation is Agree.

The overall weighted mean value of strategies to regulate Political Dynasty for respondents with monthly income of 10,000 and below is 4.09 which the verbal interpretation is Agree.

Table 28
Reasons of Existence of Political Dynasty According to Monthly Income of 11,000 to 20,000

INDICATORS	WEIGHTED MEAN	VERBAL INTERPRETATION
Political dynasty exists because of gratitude.	4	AGREE
Political dynasty exists because of money as used for political machinery.	3.96	AGREE
Members of a political family are popular because they reign for a long period of time.	4.30	AGREE
Voters trust political families because they are proven and tested by time.	4.15	AGREE
Political dynasty exists because voters have inadequate knowledge of the candidates.	3.68	AGREE
People have poor judgment in selecting officials.	3.58	AGREE
Most of the running candidates came from a political family.	4.11	AGREE
Voters believe that these political families are more knowledgeable because of their background and experiences.	3.77	AGREE
Some candidates came from wealthy and powerful families.	4.20	AGREE
The voters believe that these politicians could help them in exchange of their votes.	3.88	AGREE
OVERALL WEIGHTED MEAN	3.96	AGREE

Table 28 shows the reasons of existence of Political Dynasty for respondents with monthly income of 11,000 to 20,000

Item number 3 states that "*Members of a political family are popular because they reign for a long period of time.*" got the highest weighted mean value of 4.30 which the verbal interpretation is Agree. Item number 6 that states "*People have poor judgment in selecting officials.*" got the lowest weighted mean value of 3.58 which the verbal interpretation is Agree.

The overall weighted mean value of reasons of existence of Political Dynasty for respondents with monthly income of 11,000 to 20,000 is 3.96 which the verbal interpretation is Agree.

Table 29
Positive Effects of Political Dynasty According to Monthly Income of 11,000 to 20,000

INDICATORS	WEIGHTED MEAN	VERBAL INTERPRETATION
Political dynasties provide political stability.	3.63	AGREE
Administration of these political families were tested and proven by time.	3.79	AGREE
Members of a political family know their job more than others because of their experiences in politics.	3.61	AGREE
These politicians provide good economic performance.	3.52	AGREE
Long-term programs can be met with the help of political dynasties because there is no transmission of political power.	3.70	AGREE
Political dynasty hones an aspiring leader from a political family because children belonging in political families are being trained by their kin.	3.96	AGREE
OVERALL WEIGHTED MEAN	3.71	AGREE

Table 29 shows the positive effects of Political Dynasty for respondents with monthly income of 11,000 to 20,000

Item number 6 states that "*Political dynasty hones an aspiring leader from a political family because children belonging in political families are being trained by their kin.*" got the highest weighted mean value of 3.96 which the verbal interpretation is Agree. While, item number 4 that states "*These politicians provide good economic performance.*" got the lowest weighted mean value of 3.52 which the verbal interpretation is Agree.

The overall weighted mean value of positive effects of Political Dynasty for respondents with monthly income of 11,000 to 20,000 is 3.71 which the verbal interpretation is Agree.

Table 30
Negative Effects of Political Dynasty According to Monthly Income Of 11,000 to 20,000

INDICATORS	WEIGHTED MEAN	VERBAL INTERPRETATION
Corruption is always present.	4.41	AGREE
A political family can be a tyrant because of the power it holds.	4.12	AGREE
Political dynasties promote dirty politics because of self-serving interests.	3.95	AGREE
Political dynasty can undermine the quality of democracy by means of limiting the chances of non-dynastic to run in a position.	4	AGREE
Rural areas with a high level of political dynasties display a higher level of poverty.	3.79	AGREE
Political dynasty limits the chances of ordinary but qualified Filipinos	4.01	AGREE
OVERALL WEIGHTED MEAN	4.05	AGREE

Table 30 shows the negative effects of Political Dynasty for respondents with monthly income of 11,000 to 20,000

Item number 1 states that *"Corruption is always present."* got the highest weighted mean value of 4.41 which the verbal interpretation is Agree. While, item number 5 that states *"Rural areas with a high level of political dynasties display a higher level of poverty."* got the lowest weighted mean value of 3.79 which the verbal interpretation is Agree.

The overall weighted mean value of negative effects of Political Dynasty for respondents with monthly income of 11,000 to 20,000 is 4.05 which the verbal interpretation is Agree

Table 31
Strategies to Regulate Political Dynasty According to Monthly Income Of 11,000 to 20,000

INDICATORS	WEIGHTED MEAN	VERBAL INTERPRETATION
The Congress must define political dynasty and its content by passing the Anti-Political Dynasty Bill.	4.33	AGREE
Citizens must attend voting seminars.	4.36	AGREE
Educate people to vote more responsibly in choosing a leader.	4.08	AGREE
Limit the family members that are running for the government position.	4.25	AGREE
Concentrate on information campaign in support of non-dynastic candidates in media.	4.21	AGREE
All universities must include politics and government in their curriculum.	4.36	AGREE
OVERALL WEIGHTED MEAN	4.27	AGREE

Table 31 shows the strategies to regulate Political Dynasty for respondents with monthly income of 11,000 to 20,000

Item number 6 states that "*All universities must include politics and government in their curriculum.*" got the highest weighted mean value of 4.36 which the verbal interpretation is Agree. Item number 3 that states "*Educate people to vote more responsibly in choosing a leader.*" got the lowest weighted mean value of 4.08 which the verbal interpretation is Agree.

The overall weighted mean value of strategies to regulate Political Dynasty for respondents with monthly income of 11,000 to 20,000 is 4.27 which the verbal interpretation is Agree.

Table 32
Reasons of Existence of Political Dynasty According to Monthly Income of 21,000 and Above

INDICATORS	WEIGHTED MEAN	VERBAL INTERPRETATION
Political dynasty exists because of gratitude.	3.93	AGREE
Political dynasty exists because of money as used for political machinery.	4.17	AGREE
Members of a political family are popular because they reign for a long period of time.	4.28	AGREE
Voters trust political families because they are proven and tested by time.	3.45	NEUTRAL
Political dynasty exists because voters have inadequate knowledge of the candidates.	3.72	AGREE
People have poor judgment in selecting officials.	3.79	AGREE
Most of the running candidates came from a political family.	4.38	AGREE
Voters believe that these political families are more knowledgeable because of their background and experiences.	3.76	NEUTRAL
Some candidates came from wealthy and powerful families.	4.17	AGREE
The voters believe that these politicians could help them in exchange of their votes.	3.86	AGREE
OVERALL WEIGHTED MEAN	3.93	AGREE

Table 32 shows the reasons of existence of Political Dynasty for respondents with monthly income of 21,000 and above

Item number 7 states that "*Most of the running candidates came from a political family.*" got the highest weighted mean value of 4.38 which the verbal interpretation is Agree. While, item number 4 that states "*Voters trust political families because they are tested and proven by time.*" got the lowest weighted mean value of 3.45 which the verbal interpretation is Neutral.

The overall weighted mean value of reasons of existence of Political Dynasty for respondents with monthly income of 21,000 and above is 3.95 which the verbal interpretation is Agree.

Table 33
Positive Effects of Political Dynasty According to Monthly Income of 21,000 and Above

INDICATORS	WEIGHTED MEAN	VERBAL INTERPRETATION
Political dynasties provide political stability.	3.41	NEUTRAL
Administration of these political families were tested and proven by time.	3.38	NEUTRAL
Members of a political family know their job more than others because of their experiences in politics.	3.52	AGREE
These politicians provide good economic performance.	3.38	NEUTRAL
Long-term programs can be met with the help of political dynasties because there is no transmission of political power.	3.59	AGREE
Political dynasty hones an aspiring leader from a political family because children belonging in political families are being trained by their kin.	3.41	NEUTRAL
OVERALL WEIGHTED MEAN	3.45	NEUTRAL

Table 33 shows the positive effects of Political Dynasty for respondents with monthly income of 21,000 and above

Item number 5 states that "*Long-term programs can be met with the help of political dynasties because there is no transmission of political power.*" got the highest weighted mean value of 3.59 which the verbal interpretation is Agree. While, item numbers 2 that states "*Administration of these political families were tested and proven by time.*" And "*These politicians good economic performance.*" got the lowest weighted mean value of 3.38 which the verbal interpretation is Neutral.

The overall weighted mean value of positive effects of Political Dynasty for respondents with monthly income of 21,000 and above is 3.45 which the verbal interpretation is Neutral.

Table 34
Negative Effects of Political Dynasty According to Monthly Income of 21,000 and Above

INDICATORS	WEIGHTED MEAN	VERBAL INTERPRETATION
Corruption is always present.	4.69	AGREE
A political family can be a tyrant because of the power it holds.	4.38	AGREE
Political dynasties promote dirty politics because of self-serving interests.	4.17	AGREE
Political dynasty can undermine the quality of democracy by means of limiting the chances of non-dynastic to run in a position.	4	AGREE
Rural areas with a high level of political dynasties display a higher level of poverty.	3.83	NEUTRAL
Political dynasty limits the chances of ordinary but qualified Filipinos	3.51	AGREE
OVERALL WEIGHTED MEAN	4.10	AGREE

Table 34 shows the negative effects of Political Dynasty for respondents with monthly income of 21,000 and above

Item number 1 states that "*Corruption is always present.*" got the highest weighted mean value of 4.49 which the verbal interpretation is Agree. While, item number 6 that states "*Political dynasty limits the chances of ordinary but qualified Filipinos.*" got the lowest weighted mean value of 3.51 which the verbal interpretation is Agree.

The overall weighted mean value negative effects of Political Dynasty for respondents with monthly income of 21,000 and above is 4.10 which the verbal interpretation is Agree.

Table 35
Strategies to Regulate Political Dynasty According to Monthly Income Of 21,000 and Above

INDICATORS	WEIGHTED MEAN	VERBAL INTERPRETATION
The Congress must define political dynasty and its content by passing the Anti-Political Dynasty Bill.	4.31	AGREE
Citizens must attend voting seminars.	4.41	AGREE
Educate people to vote more responsibly in choosing a leader.	4.45	AGREE
Limit the family members that are running for the government position.	4.28	AGREE
Concentrate on information campaign in support of non-dynastic candidates in media.	4.21	AGREE
All universities must include politics and government in their curriculum.	4.41	AGREE
OVERALL WEIGHTED MEAN	4.35	AGREE

Table 35 shows the strategies to regulate Political Dynasty for respondents with monthly income of 21,000 and above

Item number 3 states that "*Educate people to vote more responsibly in choosing a leader.*" got the highest weighted mean value of 4.45 which the verbal interpretation is Agree. While, item number 4 that states "Limit the family members that are running for the government position." got the lowest weighted mean value of 4.28 which the verbal interpretation is Agree. The overall weighted mean value of strategies to regulate Political Dynasty for respondents with monthly income of 21,000 and above is 4.35 which the verbal interpretation is Agree.

The result shown on the overall mean interprets that people with monthly income of 21,000 and above suggests that there should be a strategy to regulate political dynasty by attending seminars to be knowledgeable with regards to the profile of the candidates.

The Philippines tend to elect candidates from the same set of political clans because dynastic candidates tend to come from central families in social networks, and these families have an advantage in winning office. In a recent article published in American Economic Review, Cruz, Labonne and Querubin find evidence that centrality in family networks matter a lot for the electoral success of mayoral candidates in the Philippines. Candidates from central families are not only more likely to stand for office; they also capture greater vote-shares all else equal (Ravanilla, 2017).

In other cities, one of the positive effects of Political dynasty is that programs being implemented by such families are being continued. For example in Pasig city, the city offers lots of opportunities for their inhabitants and as a result, the Local Government Unit of Pasig City received plenty of wards and citations. One of these is the Outstanding Culture Local Government Unit. The Outstanding Culture Local Government Unit is honored by the UNESCO and National Commission for Culture and Arts. This program aims to promote and develop cultural and historic places in Pasig such as Tisa House, Cave of Donya Geronima, Plaza Valentin Cruz, and Old Capitol in Barangay Sumilang, Promotion of Tourism in Pasig-Lakbay Kalesa, Lakbay-Lakad, Lakbay Group, and Lakbay Discovery Centrum Development.

In Livelihood and Employment, Pasig City offers the Following: increase market search for basket baskets / sacks from water lily and other economic products by establishing retail stores of recycled goods, building a Water Lily Processing Center, employment of students through the Summer Program for Employment Services (SPES) from 1,000 to 2,000 students, building an additional market in the area of the former Muslim Trade Center, adding loan to bad investors from P5,000 to P10,000.00, building additional BCLP and IT centers, build More Employment and Working Centers in Barangay Malinao, Maybunga, Manggahan at Kapasigan.

Dynastic politicians can learn from their political predecessors about identifying the priorities of constituents, drafting laws and getting them approved, dealing with policy compromises, and so on (Parker, 1996). Close races tend to entail more vigorous electoral campaigns (Cox and Munger, 1989), which "increase information and awareness levels within the electorate" (Geys, 2006: 648).

Ronald Mendoza, et. al. have found that dynasties thrive alongside entrenched poverty, with the presence of a greater total number of political dynasties (and larger, or "fatter," individual dynasties) correlating with more severe poverty. Studies on the direction of causality—poverty producing dynasties or dynasties producing poverty—are mixed and inconclusive; nevertheless, the AIM Policy Center's February 2014 study notes that empirical evidence suggests "stronger evidence that poverty entrenches political dynasties, and less on the reverse argument."

Indeed, critics argue that political dynasties are a symptom of deeper socio-economic conditions, and thus that the legislation and solutions needed must target the root causes. Yet, as Jan Danelle A. Patindol writes, "changing socioeconomic structures does not necessarily lead to a reduction of dynastic politics. The new forms of clan politics that may arise from evolving structures of society and the economy justify a law separate from various pieces of legislation that cater to other social and economic problems."

Some of the strategies to regulate Political Dynasty proposed in an article of Bantay Publiko are: explicitly encourage non-dynasts to contest elections at all levels, helping to address the 'supply side' of the political dynasty problem by creating a more welcoming environment and support network to lend informal guidance and insight; concentrate the already wide public support for the political dynasty prohibition into specific ancillary support for the politicians who support the bill; collaborate with the grassroots groups already advocating against political dynasties during elections by bringing to them more high-profile attention and new political parties must be incentivized to take on the responsibility of grooming and supporting non-dynast candidates, because dynasties already dominate more established parties.

5
SUMMARY OF FINDINGS, CONCLUSIONS, AND RECOMMENDATIONS

This chapter gives the summary of findings, conclusions, and recommendations of the study. This determines the perceptions of the people about Political Dynasty in Mandaluyong City.

Summary of Findings

Based on the data collected, the following are the findings:

1. Demographic profile of the Respondents

From a total of 500 participants, 49.8% of them or 249 respondents where age range from 18-35 years old, and 26.6% or 118 respondents and 23.6% or 133 respondents respectively, belonged to ages 36-45 and 46 and above. Basically, majority of the respondents were aged 18-35 years old. 42.2% of the respondents are male, while 57.8% of the respondents are female. Majority of the respondents are female. Two hundred thirty eight (238) of the respondents had a monthly income of 10,000, while 233 of the respondents had a monthly income of 11,000 to 20,000. Only 39 respondents had a monthly income of 21,000 and above. With this, it shows that majority of the respondents had a monthly income of 10,000 and below.

2. Reasons people choose the same political families

Political dynasty exists because of gratitude, money being used for political machinery. Most of the candidates came from political families who are popular because they reign for a long period of time. It can be said that, voters trust political families because they are proven and tested by time. Lastly, political dynasty exists because voters have inadequate knowledge of the candidates and poor judgment in selecting officials.

3. Positive and negative effects of the existence of Political dynasty

There were few positive effects discussed in this study. Here, the political stability brought by political dynasty is tested and proven by time. Members of a political family know their job more than others because of their experiences in politics. These politicians provide good economic performance where long-term programs can be met with the help of political dynasties because there is no transmission of political power. Also, political dynasty hones an aspiring leader from a political family because children belonging in political families are being trained by their kin. Of course corruption is always present. A political family can be a tyrant because of the power it holds and somehow promote dirty politics because of self-serving interests. It can undermine the quality of democracy by means of limiting the chances of non-dynastic to run in a position and limit the chances of ordinary but qualified Filipinos. Also, rural areas with a high level of political dynasties display a higher level of poverty.

4. Strategies to regulate the Political dynasty

Respondents ages 18 and 35 and respondents ages 46 and above believe that all universities must include politics and government in their curriculum. Respondents aged 36 to 45 think that citizens must attend voting seminars. For female respondents, citizens must attend voting seminars. For male respondents, all universities must include politics and government in their curriculum. Respondents with monthly income of 10,000 and below believe that the people should be educated to vote more responsibly in choosing a leader. On the other hand, respondents with monthly income of 11,000 to 20,000 suggest that citizens must attend voting seminars and all universities must include politics and government in their curriculum. Lastly, respondents with monthly income of 21,000 and above think that people should be educated to vote more responsibly in choosing a leader.

Conclusions

Deduce from the findings both examined and inferred, the following are the conclusion:

1. Majority of the respondents in all ages agreed on the reasons of existence of political dynasty where political and socio economic foundation is built, positive effects of political dynasty where it has shown the potential countervailing power that challenged it, and strategies that would regulate political dynasty that would effectively implement Philippine Constitutional provisions by enacting the law.

2. Majority of the respondents both male and female agree on the reasons of existence of political dynasty, positive effects of political dynasty, negative effects on political dynasty and with strategies to regulate political dynasty in Mandaluyong City.

3. Majority of the respondents by monthly income of 10,000- below, 11,000-20,000 and 21,000-above agree on the reasons of existence of y, positive effects of political dynasty, negative effects on political dynasty and with in strategies to regulate political dynasty in Mandaluyong City.

4. On the survey questionnaire, the researchers listed six (6) positive effects and six (6) negative effects of Political Dynasty. As a result, the respondents agreed to the positive effects, that Political Dynasty provides political stability and the administration of these political families were tested and proven by time because they are more knowledgeable on that field because of their experiences. Therespondents also agreed that these politicians provide good economic performance because their programs are for long term.

On the other hand, the respondents agreed to the negative effects of Political dynasty where corruption is always present. They also approve that political family can be a tyrant because of the power it holds and that promote dirty politics because of their self-interest.

This survey shows that the Political dynasty affects the community in both positive and negative ways. But on the result of our tally, the weighted means of negative effects are more predominant than the positive effects. This shows that even though citizens saw good effects of political dynasty in their community, still agree that negative effects are more rampant because of these political families.

Recommendations

Based on the following findings and conclusions, the following recommendations are set forth:

1. The persistence of political dynasty has brought adverse effects in the city including perpetuation of poverty and under development, the propagation of political and socio economic inequality and the prevalence of massive corruption. It also affects society when it comes to gender where they agree that it should be regulated in the government.

2. It is also agreed by the respondents that the local government should make strategies to regulate political dynasty, local government must effectively implement constitutional provision by enacting the law where, it could help program and projects to educate people about their voting rights.

3. Future researchers are welcome to make an in depth study too about this topic from different cities and region in the country.

4. For future studies the researchers recommend the inclusion of other variables (life elite, marginalized and the like) on their investigation that may gently affect political dynasty on the country.

References

A. Articles
Constantino, R. (1969). Emergence of Political Dynasty.
Evangelio, J. V. and Abocejo, F. T. (2015). Political Dynasty as Perceived by Residents of selected Villages in Bandian, Cebu City, Philippines, Vol 3 Issue 1.
Geys, B., and Smith, D. (2016) Political Dynasties in Democracies: Causes, Consequences, and Remaining Puzzles. Ishibashi, M., and Reed, S.R. (1992). Second-generation Diet members and democracy in Japan: Heriditary seats'. Asian Survey, vol. 32(4), pp. 366-379.
Coronel, S. (2007). The Seven Ms of Dynasty Building.
Sidel, J. (1997). Philippine Politics in Town, District, and Province: Bossism in Cavite and Cebu. Journal of Asian Studies 56(4): 947-966.
Buchanan, J. (1964). The Calculus of Consent, Royal Economic Society, DOI: 10.2307/2228407. [http://www.jstor.org/stable/2228407]
Downs, A. (1957). Rational Choice of Theory. [http://wikisum.com/w/Downs:_An_economic_theory_of_democracy, the Free Social Science Summary Database]
Paterno, B (2014). The Philippines Must Break the Power of Political Dynasties," Global Anticorruption Blog, December 2014. [https://globalanticorruptionblog.com/2014/12/01/the-philippines-must-break-the-power-of-political-dynasties/]
Ravanilla, N. (2017). The Philippines Must Break the Power of Political Dynasties," The Staying Power of Dynastic Politicians in the PhilippinesSeptember 2017.""[https://globalanticorruptionblog.com/2014/12/01/the-philippines-must-   break-the-power-of-political-dynasties/]
Simbulan, R. (2007). Political Dynasties in Mindanao, Zamboanga City. [http://www.cenpeg.org/fellows_speak/simbulan/POLITICAL_DYNASTIES_IN_MINDANAO.html]
Tadem, T. and Tadem, E. (2016). Political Dynasties in the Philippines, [http://journals.sagepub.com/doi/abs/10.1177/0967828X16659730]
Teehankee, J. (2007) And the Clans Play On. Philippine Center for Investigative Journalism [http://pcij.org/stories/and-the-clans-play-on/]
City of Mandaluyong Official Website (2017) Political History of Mandaluyong City [http://mandaluyong.gov.ph/profile/history.aspx?node=1]
Penn State News (2007) Social, Political Factors Affect Area Poverty [http://news.psu.edu/story/192067/2007/11/29/research/social-political-factors-affect-area-poverty]

B. Books

Acemoglu, D. and Robinson, J. (2006) Economic Origins of Dictatorship and Democracy. Cambridge: Cambridge University Press.

Coronel, S., et al (2003). The Rulemakers: How the wealthy and well-born dominate the Philippines. Quezon City: University of the Philippines, Department of Sociology

Dal Bo, E., P. Dal Bo and J. Snyder. 2009. Political Dynasties: Review of Economic Studies Vol. 76(1) Pages 115-142

Mccoy, A. (1994). An Anarchy of Families: State and Family in the Philippines. Manila: Ateneo de Manila University Press.

C. Theses/Research Studies

Coppenolle, B. (2014) Political Dynasties and Elections.

Guarde, E.A., Rosaroso, R., Rama, F., Batac, R., and Lasala, G. (2016) Political Dynasty in Public Governance: A Close Encounter with the Cebuanos.

Mendoza, R. and Yap, D. (2013). Political Dynasties and Poverty: Evidence from the Philippines.

Mendoza, R., et.al. (2013). Political Dynasties and Poverty: Resolving the Chicken Egg Question.

Michels, R. (1999). A Sociological Study of the Oligarchical Tendencies of Modern Democracy. Piscataway, NJ: Rutgers University

Saquibal E. and Saquibal M.L. (2016) Politics in Iloilo City: A Study of Ilonggo Perceptions On Political Patronage and Dynastic Politics In The Post-Edsa Period, 1986-2006.

Querubin, P. (2013) Political Reform and Elite Persistence: Term Limits and Political Dynasties in the Philippines.

Querubin, P. (2015) Family and Politics: Dynastic Persistence in the Philippines.

APPENDICES

Dear Respondents,

We, AB Political Science students of Rizal Technological University, would like to conduct a survey in your community for our undergraduate thesis titled, **"Political Dynasty in Mandaluyong City"**. This survey will serve as means of the researchers in determining the existence of political dynasty in Mandaluyong City. We hope for your favorable response to this request. Thank you very much!

QUESTIONS ON THE POLITICAL DYNASTY IN MANDALUYONG CITY:

DIRECTION: Please supply the needed information asked for each item. All the information in the checklist would be considered confidential.
PANUTO: Mangyaring pakibigay ang hinihinging impormasyon sa bawat aytem. Lahat ng impormasyong ilalagay sa talaan ay mananatiling pribado sa pag-aaral na gagawin.

I. Personal Background
Name: _____ (optional)
Age: _____

Gender

	Male
	Female

Monthly Income:

	10,000-Below
	11,0000-20,000
	21,000-above

Barangay

	Addition Hills		Hulo
	Bagong Silang		Mabini-J. Rizal
	Barangka Drive		Malamig
	Barangka Ibaba		Mauway

	Barangka Ilaya		Namayan
	Barangka Itaas		New Zaniga
	Buayang Bato		Old Zaniga
	Burol		Pag-Asa
	Daang Bakal		Plainview
	Hagdang Bato Itaas		Pleasant Hills
	Hagdang Bato Libis		Poblacion
	Harapin Ang Bukas		San Jose
	Highway Hills		Vergara
			Wack-wack

II. Political Dynasty in Mandaluyong City
Legend:
5- STRONGLY AGREE/ LUBOS NA SUMASANG-AYON
4- AGREE/ SUMASANG-AYON
3- NEUTRAL/ WALANG PINAPANIGAN NA PANANAW
2-DISAGREE/ HINDI SUMASANG-AYON
1-STRONGLY DISAGREE/ LUBOS NA HINDI SUMASANG-AYON

REASONS OF EXISTENCE OF POLITICAL DYNASTY	5	4	3	2	1
Political dynasty exists because of gratitude. (Mayroong political dynasty dahil sa utang na loob.)					
Political dynasty exists because of money as used for political machinery. (Mayroong political dynasty dahil sa perang ginagamit na makinarya ng mga politiko.)					
Members of a political family are popular because they reign for a long period. (Ang mga kasapi ng isang pamilyang politikal ay kilala dahil sila ay namumuno ng mahabang panahon.)					

Voters trust political families because they are proven and tested by time. (Pinagkakatiwalaan ng mga botante ang mga pamilyang political dahil sila ay subok na ng panahon.)	
Political dynasty exists because voters have inadequate knowledge of the candidates. (Mayroong political dynasty dahil hindi sapat ang kaalaman ng mga botante sa mga kandidato.)	
People have poor judgment in selecting officials. (Ang mga mamamayan ay may mababang pamantayan sa pagpili ng mga opisyales.)	
Most of the running candidates came from a political family. (Karamihan sa mga tumatakbong kandidato ay nanggaling sa pamilya ng mga politiko.)	
Voters believe that these political families are more knowledgeable in politics because of their background and experiences. (Ang mga botante ay naniniwalang mas may alam sila sa politika dahil sa kanilang pinanggalingan.)	
Some candidates came from wealthy and powerful families. (Ang ibang mga kandidato ay nanggaling sa mga mayayaman at makapangyarihang pamilya.)	
The voters believe that these politicians could help them in exchange of their votes. (Naniniwala ang mga botante na tutulangan sila ng mga ito kapalit ng kanilang boto.)	

POSITIVE EFFECTS OF POLITICAL DYNASTY	5	4	3	2	1
Political dynasties provide political stability. (Ang mga political dynasty ay nagbibigay ng balanseng pamumuno.)					
Administration of these political families was tested and proven by time. (Ang pamamahala ng mga pamilyang politikal ay subok at napatunayan na ng panahon.)					
Members of a political family know their job more than others because of their experiences in politics. (Ang mga miyembro ng isang pamilyang politikal ay may higit na kaalaman sa kanilang mga trabaho bilang lider kaysa sa iba.)					
These politicians provide good economic performance. (Ang mga opisyales ay nakakapagbigay ng maganda at aktibong ekonomiya sa kanilang komunidad.)					
Long term programs can be met with the help of political dynasties because there is no transmission of political power. (Ang mga pangmatagalan na plano ay natutupad sa tulong ng mga political dynasties.)					
Political dynasty hones an aspiring leader from a political family because children belonging in political families are being trained by their kin. (Ang naghahangad na maging isang lider na galing sa isang pamilyang political ay nahahasa dahil ang mga kabataang nabibilang sa ganitong pamilya ay isinasanay ng kanilang mga kaanak.)					

NEGATIVE EFFECTS OF POLITICAL DYNASTY	5	4	3	2	1
Corruption is always present. (Ang korupsyon ay hindi nawawala.)					
A political family can be a tyrant because of the power it holds. (Ang isang pamilya ng mga politiko ay maaaring maging isang diktador dahil sa kapangyarihan na hawak nito.)					
Political dynasties promote dirty politics because of self-serving interests. (Ang mga political dynasties ay nagpapahayag ng maduming politika dahil sa pansariling interes.)					
Political dynasty can undermine the quality of democracy by means of limiting the chances of non-dynastic to run in a position. (Ang political dynasty ay nagpapahina ng demokrasya sa kadahilanang ito ay naglilimita ng mga ordinaryong mamamayan na tumakbo sa nais na posisyon.)					
Rural areas with a high level of political dynasties display a higher level of poverty. (Ang mga probinsyang may mataas na bilang ng mga political dynasties ay nagpapakita ng mas matinding kahirapan.)					
Political dynasty limits the chances of ordinary but qualified Filipinos to serve the people because of lack of machinery. (Ang political dynasty at naglilimita sa pag-asa ng mga ordinary ngunit kwalipikadong mamamayan na maglingkod sa bayan.)					

STRATEGIES TO REGULATE POLITICAL DYNASTY	5	4	3	2	1
The Congress must define political dynasty and its content by passing the Anti-Dynasty Bill. (Ang Kongreso ay nararapat na bigyan ng tiyak na depenisyon ang Political dynasty at ang nilalaman nito sa pamamagitan ng pag-pasa ng Anti-Dynasty Bill.)					
Citizens must attend voting seminars. (Ang mga mamamayan ay narararapat na lumahok sa mga seminar tungkol sa tamang pagboto.)					
Educate people to vote more responsibly in choosing a leader. (Turuan ang mga mamamayan ng tamang pagpili at pagboto ng isang lider.)					
Limit the family members that are running for the government position. (Limitahan ang mga miyembro na tumatakbo o tatakbo para sa posisyon sa gobyerno.)					
Concentrate an information campaign in support of non-dynastic candidates on media. (Mag-pokus sa pagbibigay impormasyon sa medya hinggil sa pagsuporta sa mga hindi miyembro ng isang dinastiya.)					
All universities must include politics and government in their curriculum. (Ang lahat ng unibersidad ay dapat maglagay ng pagaaral sa politika at gobyerno sa kanilang kurikulum.)					